300

300

The
Grand Eccentrics

Art News Annual XXXII

ARTNEWS is published ten times a year, September-June;
and ARTNEWS ANNUAL [incorporating *Portfolio*],
each October, by Newsweek, Inc.
Address: 444 Madison Avenue, New York, N.Y. 10022
Telephone: TE 8-3730. Cables: Artenews, New York.

Subscription rates: Full subscription, consisting of ten
monthly issues of ARTNEWS and ARTNEWS ANNUAL,
$15.45 per year in U.S.A. Foreign postage,
$1.50 per year additional. Regular monthly issues of
ARTNEWS only, $11.50 per year in U.S.A.;
Foreign postage, $1.00 per year additional.
Single copies of ARTNEWS ANNUAL, $5.95 in U.S.A.
Foreign postage $.50 additional per copy.

ARTNEWS ANNUAL is distributed for
Newsweek, Inc. by The Macmillan Company,
60 Fifth Avenue, New York, N.Y. 10011.

European Advertising office for
Great Britain and Continental countries
Slade Fleming
ARTNEWS, 80 Haymarket, London, S.W. 1, England
Telephone: TRA 6166. Cables: Newsweek, London

Art News Annual XXXII

The
Grand Eccentrics

Five centuries of artists outside the
main currents of art history

Edited by Thomas B. Hess

Executive Editors	John Ashbery, Harris Rosenstein
Senior Editor	Henry A. LaFarge
Managing Editor	Elizabeth C. Baker
Design Director	Bradbury Thompson
Production Manager	Rena Shindelman
Production Assistant	Robert R. Preato
Publisher	Jack Fader
Advertising Manager	Roslyn E. Mandel
Circulation Manager	Alvin Garfin

The Macmillan Company, New York

The Grand Eccentrics

Contents

8

I

Eccentric Propositions

By Thomas B. Hess

Eccentric art is, by its nature, undefinable, points out Mario Praz, that passionate connoisseur of the eccentric, in another part of this volume, but are not all the various aspects of art, *sui generis,* basically undefinable? We are left with St. Wittgenstein's epistle to the art critics: continue the description—keep alive, in other words, that conversation which surrounds art and, in a sense, makes its creation easier.

And just because we seem to have entered a period when categories are once again beginning to distort and harden the dialogue, it is appropriate to talk about eccentric painting, sculpture, architecture, print-making and the various mélanges of medium on which the masters always have doted. For a long and fruitful time, the dominant modern ideas concerned an anti-ideological art that kept slipping out of pigeonholes. (Is it really Abstract-Expressionism? Or is it Action Painting? Even Harold Rosenberg, who coined the latter, unlovely handle, never seems quite positive. Or is it New York School? Post-Cubism? New-American-Style? One thing is sure; the artists followed the advice of Willem de Kooning who, in 1950, said, "It is disastrous to name ourselves."[1])

Today the labels are flooding back. Isms and movements are welcomed, not only by the fashion and gossip columnists because they add pepper to their ancedotes, but also because they seem to make easy perches upon which flocks of migratory artists can light. Nothing so necessary to a career as a label. Otherwise, how can the public know which star is where? Pop Art, Op Art, Ob Art, Top Art, Hard-Edge, Kinetics, etc.—current history seems to be relaxing back into that sputtering rhythm of action and reaction that makes freshman survey-courses of modern art so easy to memorize: Romanticism, Realism, Impressionism, Post-Impressionism, Pointillism, Expressionism, Cubism, etc.

But surely one characteristic of a serious approach is that it refuses to accept the validity of this cardboard parade which falsifies to banality what the artists were about: each man's œuvre, indeed each single painting, lives primarily as it goes beyond the boundaries of a textbook tag.

Today, on the other hand, the category tends to become the premise; to borrow a McLuhanism, the Ism is the Message. And history repeats itself, according to Karl Marx's stage-direction, as farce.

So the eccentric master becomes newly relevant and, perhaps for the first time, even exemplary, for he is, above all, the artist hostile to categories, outside of the "historical necessities" of tradition. Self-justified, he challenges all assumptions about what is possible and exposes our timidities concerning the infinite capacities of man.

As already mentioned, neither art nor any of its components are liable to definition, but there is description, and in describing, we relate. The procedure demands ground-rules, and in this anthology we have examined the great eccentric masters first of all by eliminat-

The subject of François de Nome's *King Asa of Judah Destroying the Idols* [left, cover and page 7], ca. 1625, has only recently been rediscovered. It was formerly known as *Explosion in a Cathedral,* and attributed to the so-called Monsù Desiderio [Fitzwilliam Museum, Cambridge].

John Graham: *Apotheosis* [above],
painted drawing on paper, ca. 1950,
49 inches high [Emmerich Gallery, New York].

Landes Lewitin: *Gift Bearers* [right],
1946, 30 inches high
[Royal Marks Gallery, New York].

11

ing from consideration five kinds of work which might "look" eccentric, but which adhere to very different orientations:

1. The art of the supreme masters, such as Giotto, Leonardo, Michelangelo, Rembrandt, Goya. They produced deliriously eccentric works, but they produced every other kind of work, too. In their all-encompassing nature they cut across the full spectrum of human possibilities. They are so big that they explode any argument.

2. Esoterica—arts depicting now little-known iconologies, like illustrations of gnostic texts, highly sadistic episodes of martyrdom, visualizations of scientific propositions in, for example, anatomy (dissections) or optics (extreme perspectives), mystical exercises, *mementi mori,* bizarre interior decoration and so forth. In such works, traditionalist artists use their skills to illustrate subject matter which today seems as strange as an alchemist would find the laboratories at M.I.T. But these pictures are embedded in their own pictorial continuities. Similarly, artists who have deliberately adapted eccentric subject matter to add new *frissons* to their own consistent styles are, obviously, not true eccentrics (one thinks in this connection of the Surrealists and Dadas—Picabia, Ernst, Magritte—as well as their forerunners, the sixteenth-century Mannerists of Florence, Utrecht, Fountainebleau).

3. Folk art, craftsmanship which, while it may appear inexplicable or even shocking to our eyes (Shaker dream charts, Greek ex-votos, the "palace" of the postman Cheval) nonetheless obeys its own, rigid stereotypes. In their ways, the primitive master and the artisan submit to exterior disciplines as arbitrary and as "artificial" as those of Lebrun's Academy.

4. The art of the insane which, no matter how impressive, is a mechanical process controlled by its observers—in this case alienists—just as the watercolors of apes are controlled through the selections of animal psychologists, and the art of children, by interested parents and teachers.

5. Artists who were, according to the records, eccentric or psychopathic personalities, but whose works do not reflect their interior dramas, e.g. van Gogh (a master in the high French painting tradition up to the minute before his suicide), Piero di Cosimo (who, Vasari reports squeamishly, dined off hard-boiled eggs prepared by the dozen in his gluepots), Donducci, called Il Mastelletta (painter of gentle pastorals who, according to a contemporary, was "an enemy to his friends, suspicious of all and sundry, odious even to himself, strange, unapproachable; worse, in fact, than a beast"[2]).

Seen in this narrower focus, eccentric art is no longer a mere menu of diverting subject matters, but rather an *état-d'âme* projecting through an art that is opposed to and outside the traditional, accepted, history-crowned continuities of the West. Compare an eccentric master with, for example, Henri Matisse, a "pure" painter if there ever was one, and a dedicated auto-critic. One gets the impression from studying Matisse's drawings and sketches that part of his acutely self-aware creative process was a constant censoring out of any element that might seem eccentric. He worked himself deeply into tradition, renewed it, gave it a whole new life (which even today is insufficiently comprehended, probably due to the inaccessibility of his masterworks of liberated color in the Hermitage, Leningrad). Contrariwise, it is precisely the act of the eccentric master to cut unexpectedly into, or behind, or in front of the grandly flowing stream of history. Thus, to extend the metaphor, we discover eccentrics along the edges of time, on the banks of the river, so to speak, the shoals and flats where are erected the extraordinary monuments of William Blake and Grandville, Messerschmidt and Lequeu, Seghers and Bosch, and, from our own time, the works of Frederick Kiesler, Landes Lewitin, John Graham, Joseph Cornell, Ivan Albright and a number of others. Our familiarity with them, and their closeness to our moment, should make it easier to be accurate about their motives and accomplishments, and, hopefully, to ascertain some applicable generalities.

Lichtenberg first drew the distinction between people who "believe" in something and those who find for themselves exactly the same thing. "The man," he noted, "who thinks that the moon influences the growth of plants, is ignorant, superstitious; but he who *concludes* that the moon influences their growth is a thinker, a philosopher!" The eccentric artist is, *par excellence,* the inventor. He is the man out of touch with the communications network of Style, sometimes because of his geographical distance from the center of things (e.g., the provincial nineteenth-century Americans), sometimes because of an

Lewitin: sheet of 22 working drawings, ca. 1954, colored ink and watercolor, each 3 inches high [Royal Marks Gallery, New York].

Hans Bellmer: illustration for Sade's *120 Days of Sodom,* pencil drawing, ca. 1950.

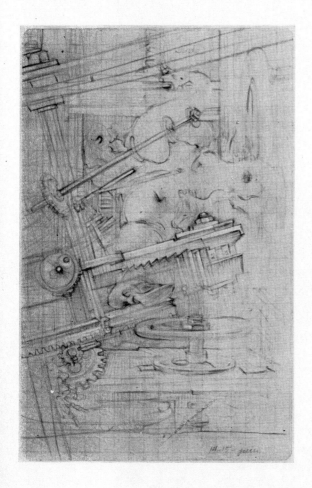

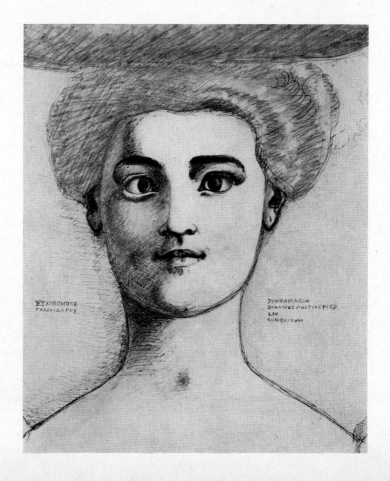

John Graham: *La Grande Duchesse "M,"* 1954, pencil and ink [Emmerich Gallery, New York].

Ivan Le Lorain Albright: *Wherefore, Now Ariseth the Illusion of a Third Dimension*, 1931 [Collection the artist].

interior, psychic distance (e.g., the thousands of metaphysical miles separating Bresdin, b. 1822, from his exact contemporary in the Paris of the early 1840s, Gustave Courbet, b. 1819).

It makes little difference to the eccentric if, as it turns out, his discovery had been patented by another years before his own enterprise began, nor if it should be inapplicable until decades after his death. His invention is a discovery of self. Edwin Dickinson's extraordinary researches in perspective and foreshortening were carried to their extreme conclusions as if Uccello, Alberti and the other Renaissance masters had never existed or, at least, as if their observations had to be endlessly reverified. And as such an invention is really a mechanism for self-discovery—for the recaptured identity—its implications are developed systematically to account for the whole self, indeed to cover the ego like a cocoon. What the traditionalist artist will accept as a hypothesis, a device or a clue, the eccentric will spin into an omnivorous cosmology. He is the artist without tactics, too busy with Grand-Designs-for-Total-Victory to bother about the intricacies of skirmish. And when he does descend to such a workaday level, it is usually to magnify each exercise to a life-or-death importance. A free-form shape for Lewitin became an imaginary letter, and the letter was extrapolated into an alphabet, and the alphabet denoted a language, and the language a secret literature which, in turn, spelled out all of human civilization.

Eccentric Propositions

The eccentric artist can entertain the wildest ambitions and be willing to adopt *any* means to accomplish his ends, because he is free of traditional imperatives, uninstructed in those areas where failure is "bound" to occur. Indeed, the posted signs which History scatters over the minefields of the contemporary feasibilities, its ultimate warning, is, "Beyond this limit lies Eccentricity."

The one concept which the eccentric artist never seems to worry about is Failure. There

Albright: *Self-Portrait at 55 East Division Street,* 1947, lithograph.

Albright: *Three Love Birds,* 1930, drawing on canvas [collection the artist].

is nothing which he cannot try—which accounts for the rich impurity of modes and mediums so characteristic of his art.

Kiesler, wanting to return architecture to its old supremacy, violently intermingled it with sculpture and painting, aiming to produce a totally organized and completely liberating (this contradiction never seems to have bothered him) environment in which art and life would fuse: pictures become walls, ceilings and floors; the "endless house" turns into sculpture; the sculpture slides back into pictures. Joseph Cornell's meticulous collage boxes are also shrines to his private cults, alluding to music, the dance, favored vaudeville stars. The constructions of Kienholz and Niki de St.-Phalle, however severe their sculptural underpinning may be, tend to blossom into the arenas of politics, morality-plays, the theater: a Scandinavian psychiatrist claims that female spectators will derive therapeutic benefit from walking into one of Niki's behemoth *Nanas* (art as healing); Kienholz' tableaux have the hortatory pressure of a soap-box speech; they yell at us "Repent!"

The very thesis that art must be pure is a history-soaked, traditionalist prejudice. Everything is grist to the anti-traditionalist's mills. The point of Paul Greenwood's extraordinary *Grande Odalisque* is its fantastical interrelationship of parts at an eerie slightly over-life-size scale, but in order to heighten the naturalistic shock, he commissioned local Philadelphia milliners to manufacture a "real" costume for his epoxy goddess. It is an idea which, Western art history will instruct the artist over and over again, simply cannot work. Greenwood's grand, hallucinatory image does work, in a sense, as it mocks such lessons.

Edwin Dickinson's beautiful *Ruin at Daphne* hangs in the Metropolitan Museum as serenely as any Chardin, but, as Elaine de Kooning pointed out in her essay on the artist,[3] it has a whole scenario which informs and justifies (to the artist, of course; it is a private matter) each detail. It depicts a building which was first a "Roman ruin in Syria, built 40 A.D.," with a "concoction of corrupted Corinthian, Doric and Ionic" . . . In 1600, a

Eccentric
Propositions

Joseph Cornell: Untitled box (doll with spider), mid-1940s, 18½ inches high [Allan Stone Gallery, New York].

Lucas Samaras: Untitled box, 1966, mixed mediums [Pace Gallery, New York].

Red Grooms: *Loft on 26th Street* [above], 1965-66, mixed medium construction, 30½ inches high [de Nagy Gallery, New York].

Joe Brainard: *Japanese City* [below], 1965, assemblage [Alan Gallery, New York].

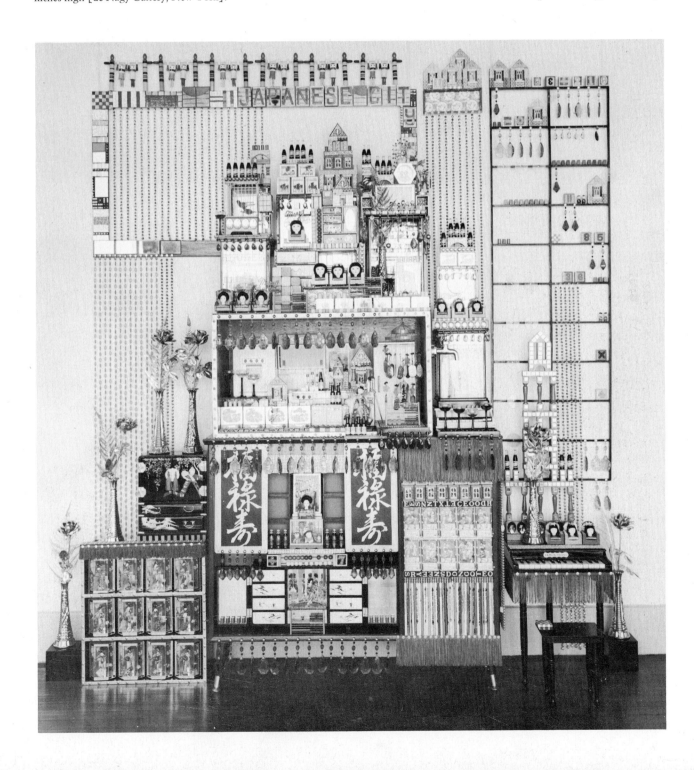

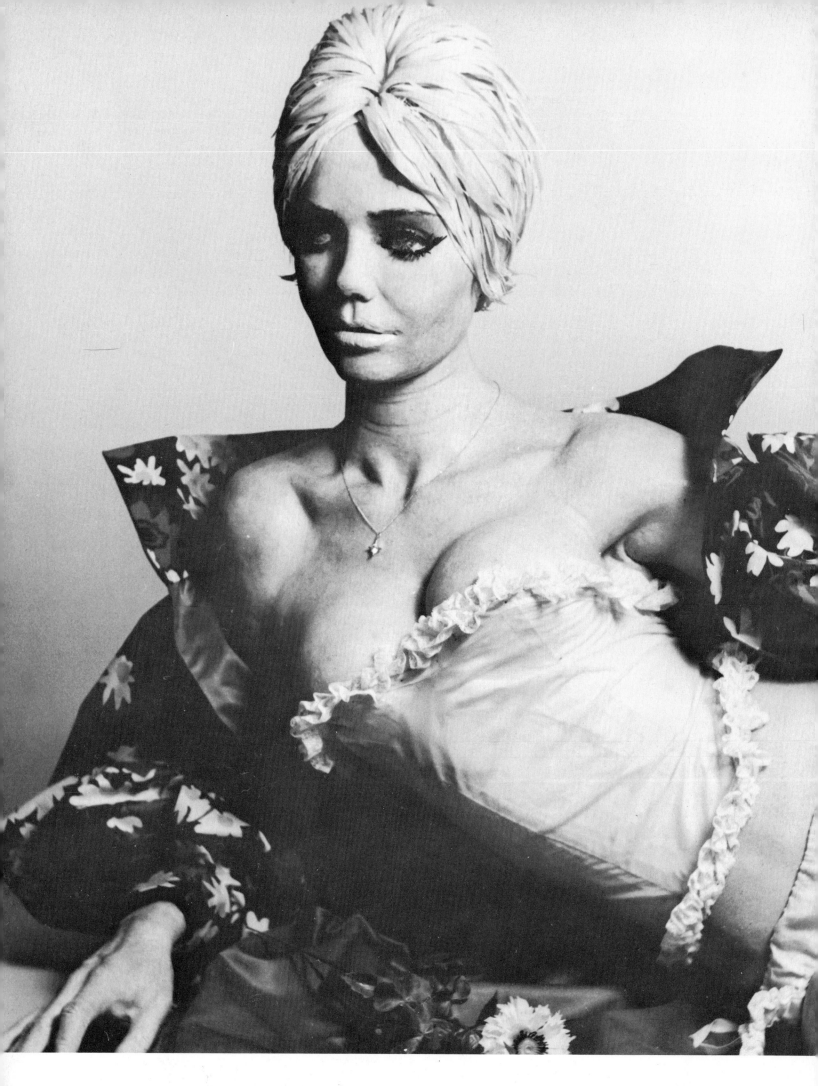

silo with a covered shaft leading up to it was added . . . "In 1900, the ruin was bought by a well-to-do Frenchman who landscaped it and built a pool." In other words, Dickinson's Art itself cannot justify the distortions of a shape or an anachronism; his image grows from a subsoil of fiction which gives to each detail a demonstrable veracity.

One sometimes wonders in this connection whether Kandinsky's abstractions of the 1930s, with their mystical assumptions of musical surrogates and theosophical atmospherics, will not be seen by future generations as works apart from the tradition of developing abstraction (where they are set so firmly today), as eccentricities more related to Moreau than to Mondrian.

With his high ambition, scorn of failure, willingness to take any risks to achieve his vision, the eccentric is not only quick to slice through the mediums and protocols, but, to emphasize a point, he will often accumulate his effects into monumental conglomerations. There is a kind of Tower-of-Babel aspect to this art, a piling up of details, as if to reach Heaven by sheer work. Lucas Samaras' constructions grow until they fill a whole room; the smaller the unit (and with Samaras, it is the pinpoint), the wider its proliferation. In one of his exhibitions he included his complete bedroom, and not only because he wanted a month of rent-free living. His work seems to flow along lines of accelerating self-reproduction. Joe Brainard's *Japanese City* rejoices in similar polyphiloprogenitive energies. The gimcrack parts (artificial flowers that would make an undertaker weep; beads that Sadie Thompson would consider *outré*), as they are repeated and multiplied, take on a severe gothic radiance.

The eccentric's pack-rat instinct, his refusal to give anything up, is the trait which most often lights a glint of superior recognition in the eye of the psychiatrically inclined observer. He recognizes obsessional behavior when it hits him over the head, and the whiffs of paranoia. To a certain extent, he is right. If artists are to be parceled out among the bins

Eccentric Propositions

Paul Anthony Greenwood: *La Grande Odalisque* [above, and detail left], 1963-66, epoxy and clothes.

Paul Thek: Untitled sculpture [right], 1966, wax, plexiglass, formica, rhodium-plated bronze, 19 inches high [collection Robert D. Brown].

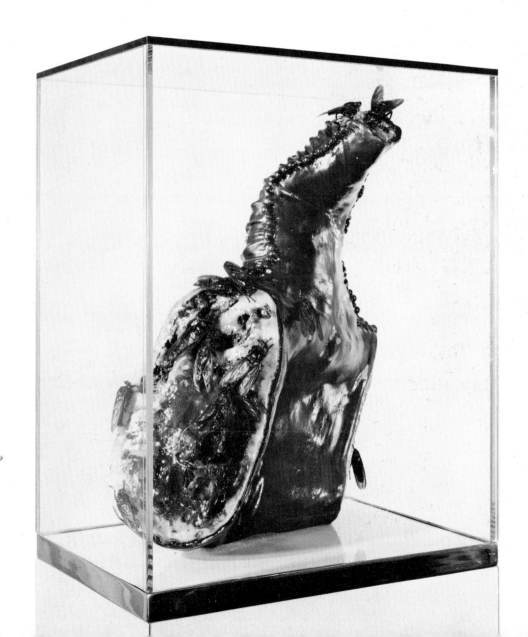

Louis Eilshemius: *Jealousy,*
1915 [above; collection Mr. and Mrs.
Henry Clifford, Philadelphia].

Niki de Saint-Phalle: *Teenie,* 1965,
mixed mediums, 20 inches high
[below; Iolas Gallery, New York].

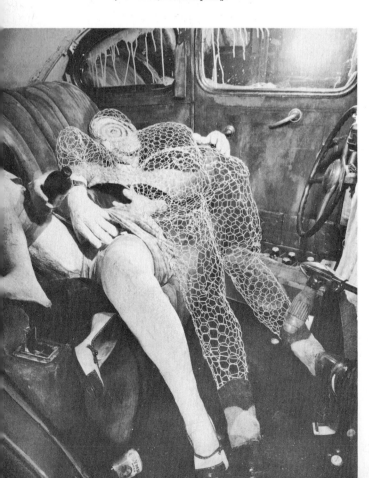

Edward Kienholz: *Back Seat Dodge,* 1964,
tableau in mixed mediums, 5½ feet
high [detail, left; Dwan Gallery, New York].

of amateur psychology, it is the eccentrics who, more than any other, come out as looneys (but this is only for amateur psychologists; Freud himself warned professional colleagues that the artist is always the major exception to Freudian generalities).

The eccentrics tend to repeat an obsessional theme over and over again. This rhythm will also affect their methods. Joseph Cornell, for example, has boxes of classified esoteric material for his constructions, and his fragile, exquisitely calculated objects—precious in the noblest sense of the word—are produced on what amounts to a home-factory assembly-line. Lewitin made tens of thousands of drawings which he kept in suitcases and laundry-boxes, sorted according to size. A picture of a dog and a bird would reappear, over the years, on a bit of paper the size of a thumbnail, and in larger and larger sizes up to 7 feet. Lewitin was also deeply involved with color effects and would discourse learnedly, for hours, on the chemistry of certain lilac and leaf-green hues. In order to increase their intensity, he first combed the paint; later he attempted to arrive at a maximum surface exposure to light by mixing tiny glass balls with his pigment. The Surrealist Hans Bellmer, the one artist of the circle who seems to have been genuinely haunted by his subject matter, made thousands of fine-line pencil drawings of an erotic doll with (sadistically) demountable parts that he had constructed to his own peculiar specifications. And the more familiar he became with his model, from years of drawing it, the more exalted became his graphic technique.

Eccentric Propositions

But is not this saliently obsessional quality in eccentric art an indication not of its strangeness, but precisely where it has a common ground with the great tradition? The recurring theme is omnipresent through history—Matisse's mirror-image and a certain saturated blue; Ingres' long-spined odalisque; Dürer's line with a hook to its end. The artist is the old dog who goes back to his bone, who never forgets, who always seeks to recapture the one incandescent experience (which maybe never happened at all) when art and idea were one. What the eccentric is apt to do is to expose the search. He cares nothing about the public (or misjudges it so badly that it is the same thing as not caring) and proudly or naïvely refuses to disguise his anxieties and passions. For the traditionalist, such revelations would throw off-kilter the whole precarious balance of style and the decorum style implies. The eccentric does not fret about revealing himself because he is, supremely, the artist without a mask. If he is a gourmet of deliquescence, or a gourmand like Ivan Albright, this leaning dominates the whole approach to his art and also to his technique.

The traditionalist artist will shuffle his quirks with those common to his time; it is impossible to tell which is which. Was Carpaccio a necrophiliac, or Gros? Or did they share with the Zeitgeist a fascination for corpses in various stages of decay? The equilibrium of their art makes it impossible for us to move beyond a trivial guess. But with John Graham or Paul Thek, art is not a matter of balancings, but of self-revelations. One is tempted to suggest a formula:

For the artist in the tradition, the image tends to merge with Art.

For the eccentric, the image tends to merge with Life.

For the former, the deeper one looks, the more trivial becomes the biography of the artist. (Who cares if Giotto was happily married or if Watteau was an atheist?)

For the latter, the deeper one looks, the more biographical details are needed to explain the image. (We cannot fully understand Bosch by line, color and form; it becomes essential to understand his system, and his attitude towards it.)

Red Grooms's assemblages, for example, like some of Samaras', tended to be resumés of his daily life, climaxed in 1966 by a meticulously painted replica of his studio—a souvenir of a Chelsea loft from which he had been evicted, with every book, pin-up and casserole recorded in cheerfully fanatic miniaturization. One has only to compare this evocation of the artist's life with Courbet's *Atelier* or Matisse's *Red Studio* (in the Hermitage)—or, if this relationship seems a bit high-flown, with Alex Katz's *Cocktail Party* or Elaine de Kooning's portrait gallery of the artist's friends—to recognize the peculiar advantages and dangers of Grooms's eccentricity. Alex Katz and Elaine de Kooning, eminently "concentric" painters, create pictures in which the models, their scale, the light and space they breathe, insistently refer to their "virtual" existence in paint. It makes little difference if we know, or ignore, the fact that this man is Edwin Denby or that one is Merce Cunningham. In Grooms's studio, the *roman* is incomplete without its *clef*. The strangeness of scale which Grooms's little pop-up characters share with Greenwood's amazon, the transposition of the colors of nature into their symbols in pigment, the concentration on details which raises crankiness to an epic plane, move this art away from Art—to a different realm, where another magic is invoked.

The eccentric, then, works apart, in a different esthetic, which he has systematized to express his own personality as forcefully as possible. What Virgil Thompson has written about virtuosity, in fact, seems to be more applicable to eccentricity, a situation in which artists "do not grow like vital organisms, but rather, like crystals, reproduce their characteristic forms." And Stendhal's metaphor for love also applies—falling in love, he explained, is a process of crystallization, and the eccentric artist has fallen in love with himself. He is the unalienated individual, uninterested in the continuities of avant-garde rebellion: the Compleat Angler.

Why then, of all artists, does the eccentric seem to be most influenced by his environment? Traditional artists move with charmed lives through times of chaos. Cities are sacked, the countryside is devastated, plagues decimate the population, the government falls to the barbarians, and the artist continues his work, like the plowman in Breughel's *Icarus,* huge in his huge landscape, totally oblivious to a pair of tiny pale legs disappearing into the wide sea.

In certain societies, for example, the eccentric artist simply does not exist—in tribal, or in closed homogeneous communities. Eccentricity is unthinkable in Dynastic Egypt, in early and Classic Greece, among the Romanesque cathedrals or Medici piazzas. Is it because, in such an environment, the eccentric work is destroyed as soon as it appears? Or does it not appear at all, and reserve its coming to times of dissolution, wrenching change, when man is suddenly thrown back on himself—like Bosch at the end of the Middle Ages, François de Nome in seventeenth-century Naples, Fuseli at the confluence of the Romantic and Neo-Classic tides, the fin-de siècle French Decadents, our contemporaries in the Aspirin or Atomic Age? Perhaps being in the tradition immunizes, in a way, the classical artist from the poisons of his times, leaving him free to work? And are DNA spirals so coded that at certain purposive moments, at the crises, there will be a production of

Eccentric Propositions

Frederick Kiesler: *Horse Galaxy,* 1954, painted and constructed environment, 10 feet high [left; photo shows installation in Janis Gallery, New York].

Kiesler: *Kiesler and Goya,* 1965, painted, constructed and sculpted environment, incorporates Kiesler's version of Goya's *Burial of the Sardine* sketched on a convex panel, rough-hewn wood beams and Kiesler's gleaming bronze bone-form [right; Jackson Gallery, New York].

mutants? All we have is the paradox of the freest men being held most tightly in the clasp of History.

Perhaps this sense of being controlled, preordained, is what makes so many eccentric masters rail against their milieux. The classic artist accepts them: no sooner does the automobile become a part of the landscape than Matisse incorporates it into his vision. The eccentric fights, looks away, sometimes to a distant past which will be recovered through arcane practices: Messerschmidt felt he had discovered the "Egyptian" secrets of proportion; John Graham, of a chivalric alchemistry. Sometimes the future is entailed, with astonishingly prophetic results: after the appearance of Abstract-Expressionism, a whole series of very free Action Paintings by Gustave Moreau were found in the museum he willed to the State. Forrest Bess, who makes his living as a shrimp fisherman in Texas, who also writes Jungean tragedies, has produced over the years a series of hyper-sensitive little visionary canvases; in one of them he accurately predicted the shape and performance of Sputnik several years before the Russians invented the space-craft.

And like prophets, the eccentric artists are usually unhonored. Fighting against their civilizations, they end up being treated as enemies, exiled to a solitary life. They suffer extreme loneliness and bitterness at lack of recognition, which often results finally in mental collapse. The case of Louis Eilshemius can be considered a characteristic exception. Out of a rather academic late-Barbizon style, he evolved his visionary landscapes peopled with highly sexed nudes and theatrical scenes of melodramatic violence. Alone in his belief in his greatness, he went through the humiliation of being briefly "discovered" by the Dadas and finally died, a hermit in his own house, imprisoned by an unbelievable accumulation of pictures, music scores, handbills, newspapers, assorted and unassorted junk.

However the final revenge which history takes on the artists who defy it is to obliterate their names. For generations Seghers, father of the polychrome engraving, was forgotten and his paintings dispersed under Rembrandt's label. Fuseli, like Eilshemius, became a ghost in his own lifetime. How many readers are familiar with Lequeu or Romako? The example of François de Nome bears retelling. For years a number of anonymous paintings of sweeping birds-eye panoramas and cataclysms in churches were preserved in the cellars of museums in Vienna and Naples. Then, as scholars, notably L. Réau, A. Scharf and R. Causa, began to study them, certain names emerged from documents and darkened inscriptions. The first was that of "Monsù Desiderio." At this juncture, Prof. Causa explains, strange things began to happen. The wing of the building in which the Naples pictures were stored kept catching fire. Photographers sent to document them found their lenses shattered, tripods buckling; one technician broke his leg. The pictures of Monsù Desiderio became infamous for a singularly virulent *malocchio* ("The Evil Eye is ridiculous," said Croce, "but it exists"). Finally the true authors were discovered, two artists from Metz who had worked in Naples, Didier Barra, who executed the panoramas, and François de Nome, master of exploding cathedrals.[4] "The paintings seemed urgently to desire their proper names," said Prof. Causa, "and now that the mystery is solved, they are at rest." But while he told the story, he kept his left hand in the propitiatory double-horn gesture.

The art itself fights back. Is the recovery of so much eccentric art in the last fifty years due to the expanding disciplines of art history, or also because our century has a special need for its examples? It teaches the strength that comes from humiliation and the purity (in all these impurities) of one man attempting a full expression of his interior reality.

The eccentric may shun the crises of Art and, by ignoring real issues, doom himself to produce relatively minor work (in spite of his over-reaching ambitions). But if his back is turned to Art, he faces squarely the Existentialistic crisis of Man. And he triumphs through his own absurd, obsessed, tragi-comic heroism.

Perhaps we would sacrifice a hundred eccentric pictures for one grand Titian? But would we relinquish one eccentric artist? The argument keeps coiling back *ad hominem*. The artists come first because they are the true guardians of the very spirit of man, that fallen angel—whose motto is Lucifer's "I shall not serve."

Eccentric Propositions

Forrest Bess: *Prophecy,* 1946, 6 inches high, is a vision of a proto-Sputnik, painted years before the fact [above, left; collection Meyer Schapiro, New York].

Edwin Dickinson: *Ruin at Daphne,* 1943-53, 48 inches high [below, left; Metropolitan Museum, New York].

[1] Quoted in a round-table discussion published in *Modern Artists in America,* N. Y., 1951.
[2] Malavasia, quoted in *Born Under Saturn* by Rudolf and Margot Wittkower, N. Y., 1963, p. 116f., an extremely valuable study, filled with knowledge and common-sense, of artists' temperaments, aberrations and their inter-actions with the environment.
[3] *Dickinson Paints a Picture;* ARTNEWS, Sept., 1949.
[4] *Didier Barra et François de Nome dits Monsù Desiderio,* by Felix Sluys, Paris, 1961.

Edwin Dickinson: *The Fossil Hunters*, 1926-28,
96½ inches high [Whitney Museum, New York].

Joseph Cornell: Untitled box, late 1950s,
18 inches high [Allan Stone Gallery, New York].

II

The Visionary French

By Michael Benedikt

Author

Michael Benedikt, poet and art critic, specializes in turn-of-the century French avant-garde manifestations. His anthology of French theater from Jarry to Ionesco appeared in 1964. His newest volume, on postwar German theater, will come out this winter, and one on 20th-century American imaginative drama is in preparation.

Odilon Redon's charcoal drawing, *Day*, 1891, teems with ghostly bits of ectoplasm [Galerie Bateau Lavoir, Paris].

"The artists of my generation, for the most part, have looked at a chimney flue and have seen only a chimney flue." With that complaint the great French lithographer, etcher and painter, Odilon Redon, placed the primary impulses of his period in a perspective from which the work of the more bizarre artists of the later nineteenth century, Redon included, was to prove a happy and influential escape. Their work proved significant for the future as well as for the health of the period. In speaking of Redon's "period" we of course bracket a considerable sweep of time. Yet, from the tough, hard-headed Realism of Courbet or the somewhat more evasively realistic painting of Corot to the painting flourishing in Redon's later years, the general current is clear: Naturalism. Indeed, it is touchingly symptomatic of the mid-nineteenth-century situation that in the series of newspaper articles Redon wrote on the Salon of 1868, at which the Impressionists exhibited *en masse,* he, almost alone, should have praised them. For all their incipiently scientific technique, these painters were daring to set up shop at a definite—albeit optical—distance from reality and its immediate pressures.

Still, as Redon knew, his own work meant more: a force in a new direction. The distinction of Redon and his few confrères among mid- and late-nineteenth-century French artists lay not just in an ability to disperse optically the outlines of chimneys, but to see in them hints of altogether other worlds—in short, to impose a personal vision. Unchristened to this day, Redon and his fellow visionaries form a group parallel to the Symbolist poets who enlivened with personal, extra-earthly imagery the literature of the time. For their intentions, and in some cases for their achievement, we can place beside the names of Baudelaire, Nerval, Gautier, Rimbaud, Verlaine, Corbière, Mallarmé, those of Redon, Grandville, Bresdin, Moreau, the Belgian Ensor, and, for his little-known drawings, the great poet Victor Hugo.

What linked these artists? Aside from a mutual enthusiasm for the visionary, there are examples of definite inter-influence, and even friendship. A firmer common denominator was a fascination with literature and an inclination to draw upon it as a source of visions and inspiration. The necessity for extra-painterly inspiration was, indeed, becoming increasingly apparent around 1865, the year Redon first began to exhibit. Romanticism's most powerful impulse, which had been toward the exploration of the exotic, often in connection with exacerbated emotional states, was gradually being diffused and lost. This loss was manifest not only in France, but throughout the empire of Romantic art. Delacroix continued to paint, but while he was achieving increasing economy in structure and originality of color, his visions broke no new ground. His paintings of North Africa, his work inspired by the Bible, or the writings of Shakespeare and Goethe, had themselves begun to look like classics long before his death in 1863. They decorated state buildings; Prime Minister Thiers himself was a fan.

Appropriately enough, it remained for a champion of the art of Delacroix, and also the first of the Symbolists, Charles Baudelaire, to urge a painting which would take

literature into account—not necessarily for the sake of literature, but rather for the visionary imagery such painting often resulted in: "From day to day art diminishes its self-respect, prostrates itself before exterior reality, and the artist becomes more and more inclined to paint not what he dreams but what he sees . . . the great tradition has been lost, and the new one has not yet been made."

Indeed, simply for a poet to devote himself so seriously and at such great length to art criticism provided a revolutionary example. Further implications appear throughout his masterwork, *Les Fleurs du Mal,* which frequently uses phenomena found in the other arts: light, color, patterning, even sounds, smells. In one poem he wrote of Delacroix in a manner more visionary than Delacroix himself:

Delacroix, lac de sang hanté des mauvais anges,
Ombragé par un bois de sapins, toujours vert . . .

"Les parfums, les couleurs, et les sons se répondent," he announced in his famous *"Correspondances,"* regarding the possible equivalence of the senses in a new visionary whole.

The Visionary French

The work of one of the great nineteenth-century masters of the dream vision, Jean Ignace-Isidore Gérard, known as Grandville, seems nevertheless to have taken even Baudelaire by surprise. "There are superficial individuals whom Grandville 'diverts'; as for me, he positively frightens . . . this man, with a superhuman courage, spent his life re-creating creation," Baudelaire noted. This *"nouveau frisson"* was produced by a man who was a designer by profession, but who soon graduated into cartooning, which

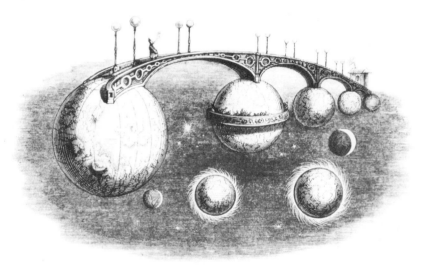

Two illustrations from Grandville's fantastic tale, *Un Autre Monde,* 1844, approximately actual size: A series of Parisian-style bridges linking the planets [left]; one pier rests on Saturn whose rings become a crowded circular balcony; and a group of admirers of an unknown beauty [below] is literally, and frighteningly, all "eyes."

Odilon Redon: *Christ and the Serpent,* 28 inches high [Silberman Gallery, New York].

he at first practised to considerable acclaim for various newspapers. For a while, in the 1830s, he worked with Daumier on *Charivari*. Like many caricaturists during the reign of Louis-Philippe, he attacked the ruling group with a savagery which had to be qualified by a certain obliqueness, due to relatively strict censorship. Like many others, Grandville chose frequently to render familiar political figures as beasts, fusing human head and animal body, and vice-versa. Some of his first books generalized the imagery, and illustrated assorted texts by various mostly forgotten writers with fanciful drawings of animals in human garb. Grandville's first great book, *Les Métamorphoses du Jour* (1829), was politico-satirical in intention, but subsequent works involving hybridization aimed straight at strangeness. Grandville usually created his drawings in connection with the literary works of others: the nearly anonymous cliché, the proverb, the jingles of Béranger, a child's ABC, the fables of La Fontaine were among his initial texts. Only occasionally— as in the illustration of a sequence of noses, moustached, warted, bespectacled, carbuncled, enormous, etc., hung up on a clothesline *(Mémoires d'un Nez* from *Les Petites Misères de la Vie Humaine* by a writer known as "Old Nick")—are there hints of the later imaginative flarings. Grandville's masterpiece is undoubtedly *Un Autre Monde* (1844), a book with both illustrations and texts by the artist. One of the charms of his fanciful imagination is its frequent basis in a disarming literalness: the title is prefigured by one of the artist's earlier illustrations in which a series of bridges, such as he knew in Paris, link a series of planets like islands. It is hard to say whether illustrations or texts are more extraordinary; or, indeed, which medium dictated which. It would seem, however, judging from Grandville's usual use of literature as inspiration, that tale usually preceded illustration. However, in an introductory conversation between a pen and pencil, the pencil (probably representing the artist's own feelings) announces his intention to take the place of the writer's pen, and compose a travel book. The story that follows is a fantastic tale of three caricature Frenchmen (named Puff, Hahblle and Kraackq—suggesting a possible kinship with Poe's *Hans Phaall,* a fantastic tale issued in 1840). They decide, logically, that since only gods can set forth freely to seek the new and extraordinary, they must declare themselves "neo-gods." The illustrations seem to force the innocence of the text into fantastic arenas. One of the three men attends an opera; the door of one of the boxes opens and a beautiful lady appears. "Instantly all eyes turned toward her . . . one eye, it must have been an academician's eye, exclaimed 'She is Venus herself. . . .' I looked passionately into her face, and she seemed to smile." The illustration scrupulously and shockingly follows the text. It pictures a typical fashion-plate beauty of the period undergoing the rapt scrutiny of an audience of men whose heads are eyes, mounted above high starched collars; individuals literally "all eyes"—veins, lashes and all. Despite the playfulness of his attack, his light-hearted representation of literary fantasies and his popularity, Grandville's spiritual isolation during this particular period must have been formidable. It may well be that he paid for his visionary excursions dearly: he died mad in 1848.

Victor Hugo's visionary-literary art had, at least, a certain cachet: for his poetry fairly early in his life became the nationally respected monument which it is today. Indeed, Hugo's poetry seems less remarkable now, when placed next to that of such prototype Symbolists as Nerval and Baudelaire, than even his very first sketches do, when placed next to the work of most of the artists of his era. The difference is understandable. As a poet Hugo was a fervent classicizer, an explorer of a technique that had already been established, and which he was not to leave appreciably varied for all the genuinely revolutionary Romanticism of his sentiments. As an artist, he was an amateur. His first sketches, like Grandville's satirical drawings, were done during the '20s—around the time that his first poems (*Nouvelles Odes,* 1824), plays (*Hernani,* 1830) and novels (*Notre-Dame de Paris,* 1831) also appeared. Hugo's more serious, unsatirical graphic productions roughly parallel these early works with their evocations of Gothic horror and Romantic yearning. His drawings of this period picture blasted plains above which rise the steeples and towers of fantastic cities; mysterious barques in mythical medieval harbors; hanged men dangling from architecture or, odder yet, in the middle of a bleak field; an enormous mushroom may sprout in the center of a plain, or a quartet of sirens surface from a pond. Hugo eventually began to experiment with techniques, particularly a Rorschach-like method of improvising images from the suggestions of random flowings of ink or casual shiftings and foldings of paper. His final drawings added disembodied arms, shrieking wide-eyed heads, sea-monsters, harpies and other infernal imagery to the commoner

The Visionary French

Interlaced initials of Juliette Drouet and Victor Hugo, and view of Marine Terrace (in Jersey, where Hugo spent much of his political exile); 1855, ink and gouache, 16 inches high [Collection Mme. R. Langlois-Berthelot]. *A more disguised recurrence of the letter "H" appears in the composition of* City at the Broken Bridge [lower right].

Victor Hugo: *Elegant Group on Stairs,* pen and bistre wash, 9¼ inches high [Schaeffer Galleries, New York]. The dramatic, spotty illumination exemplifies Hugo's fascination with the "battle between light and shadow."

Hugo's *City at the Broken Bridge,* sepia wash and ink, 7 inches high [Musée Victor Hugo, Paris], is typical of his outpouring of medieval architectural fantasies which earned him the nickname "Hugoth."

exotica of the earlier pictures. Among his last drawings are sketches of astral bodies drifting in space—an indication that Hugo had not only been meditating on his own *Légende des Siècles* (1877), but also the recently published astronomical speculations of Flammarion, which were also to influence Redon. Baudelaire, who was relatively half-hearted about Hugo's literary works (which he tended to see as too preachy in regard to acts of charity), sent Hugo unqualified compliments on his drawings, together with a copy of his own *Salon of 1859.* Hugo wrote back with excessive modesty that he just wanted to "reflect in a way something which is in my eye and above all in my spirit." Then, resuming the tones of *Le grand Victor,* the poet added professionally: "I just dash them off between stanzas."

Concerning Rodolphe Bresdin, Baudelaire appears to have been even more whole-heartedly enthusiastic than he had been toward the modest Hugo, or toward Grandville, who seemed to astonish him by the directness of his attack ("It is as an artist, rather than a craftsman, that he interests me"). Bresdin could please on two accounts: a revolutionary and visionary image-maker, he was also, as a print-maker, a masterful technician. In one of his efforts to introduce Bresdin to some of his influential Paris acquaintances, Baudelaire directed a word of introduction to his old friend and fellow connoisseur of modern painting, Théophile Gautier: "Do welcome Bresdin as an *old* acquaintance; perhaps you will feel that way about him after you have seen his work." (Gautier followed Baudelaire's advice, and his poem *"La Comédie de la Mort"* is based on one of Bresdin's greatest works and dedicated to the artist.) As much as Bresdin's hand had been steadied by devotion to print-making, his eye had been illuminated by literature. Bresdin expressed both his contempt for earthly realities and his will to achieve a distinction in traditional terms by ceaselessly sketching not merely biblical figures—as Delacroix and other Romantics had—but biblical and other mythical figures uncomfortably out of place (and time), wandering in a helpless and penurious exile. Redon's description captures the spirit of the work nicely: "What we find everywhere, almost from the beginning to the end of his work, is Man enamored of solitude, fleeing desperately under a sky, in the anguish of a hopeless and unending exile. This dream, this constant anxiety, appears in the most diverse shapes. Sometimes it is in the form of the divine Child, in the Flight into Egypt, so often treated by the artist. At times it is a whole family, a legion, an army, a whole people fleeing, always fleeing, from civilized humanity."

Whether Bresdin was rendering fantastic wanderers, or soldiers with helmets and lances mingling among rocky peaks, or unsuspecting bathers spied upon by concealed skeletons, or interiors with drinkers and serving-girls crammed together in merriment, there is a tendency toward teeming. Unexpected and gargoylesque details proliferate; often a magnifying glass is not only helpful, but necessary for a full examination. Sometimes even the central figures of his biblical wanderer works must be picked out from the profuse leafy backgrounds which seem to threaten more than shelter them; details suggesting bodies, eyes or entire monsters lurk in the landscape; entire cities occupy the space of an inch. Even skies, in Bresdin's world, are curly with arabesquing cloud formations in a curious dotted-line script; often sprinkled with birds, they crown his work with passages of the greatest elaborateness and visionary intensity. It is interestingly true that such celebrated prints as *The Good Samaritan, The Comedy of Death* and several of the series of *Holy Families* are today considered, for their technique alone, masterworks of nineteenth-century print-making. Still, for Bresdin, the sense of the other world, or the longing for it, appears to have been crucial. The few prints which one can call weak are usually those in which the central subjects dominate: in which the human outline is seen up close, writ large—unthreatened by nightmare foliage, rocks or peering chimeras. Bresdin actually spent a large part of his adult life in or near Bordeaux, from where he hoped to embark for "another world"—America. (His actual journey to America —originally inspired by reading Fenimore Cooper's *The Last of the Mohicans* 20 years before—ended badly, with Bresdin in deeper poverty than ever before.) Indeed, the unique genius of his prints is that in them the artist considers wandering as a permanent condition.

For Gustave Moreau, there appears never to have been any question of departure, except in imagination. "I believe neither in what I touch nor in what I see," Moreau noted. "I believe only in what I sense. Only my inner feelings seem to me eternal and incontestably certain." Moreau's subjects, practically from the first, were entirely visionary. From early copies of his hero, Delacroix, he moved immediately to versions of religious

Odilon Redon: *Salomé*, pastel,
22⅜ inches high [Schweitzer Gallery, New York].

Bresdin's obsessive, delicate tangle of
line materializes into *The Tree,* 6½ inches
high [Galerie Bateau Lavoir, Paris].

Macabre subjects dominate much of Bresdin's
œuvre: *Nightmare,* india ink drawing, 7⅛
inches high [Metropolitan Museum, New York].

legends: his Salon debut in 1852 was made with a *Pietà*. After a period in Italy studying Renaissance painting he also concentrated on rendering the myths of literary antiquity: the canvas which brought him recognition, creating a stir at the 1864 Salon, was his first *Oedipus and the Sphinx*. By this time Moreau's central preoccupation is plain: the dangerous and dominating Fatal Woman. More than half the *oeuvre* portrays triumphant and savage Circe, Salomé, Helen, Delilah, Herodiade, etc. Moreover, even in Moreau's work consecrated to the hero or the tragic poet, these central males stand confronted crushingly by womankind or her unconquerable surrogate imagery: Oedipus stands before the Sphinx, Orpheus is beleaguered and St. John decapitated, repeatedly. Indeed, perhaps only literature, and a process of careful personal anthologization, could have provided a so consistently sinister collection of females.

Although Moreau confined himself to classicized visions of his obsession, its spirit was abundantly present in contemporary literature. As Mario Praz shows in *The Romantic Agony,* the ideal of the Fatal Woman is a touchstone, if not the central theme, of much late Romantic and Symbolist literature. Moreau was an ardent Wagnerite, even boasting that he could sing parts of all his operas. The painter's great theme sounds forth not only in the German composer's libretti, but also in such writers among Wagner's contemporaries as Heine ("In woman one never knows clearly where the angel leaves off and the devil begins"), Schopenhauer ("Every hero is a Samson"); and among writers Moreau may well have known personally, in Vigny ("And, more or less, every woman is Delilah"), Nerval (*Les Chimères,* a celebrated sonnet-sequence on mysterious ladies of 1854, is echoed in Moreau's multi-ladied *The Chimeras*), as well as Baudelaire ("Woman is the antithesis of the spiritual"). Among the Romantic poets, it is Baudelaire who was the most ingenious and insistent exponent of the myth. The poet (who died in 1867) even seems to foreshadow in his ideal of beauty the two principles upon which Moreau insisted: "Necessary Richness" and "Beautiful Inertia." "Of every human being he makes a piece of jewelry covered with jewelry," Gauguin wrote of Moreau's first principle. This remark is apt in two senses: not only does Moreau create an amazingly rich, choked surface in his paintings, but he is also gorgeously elaborate when he depicts costumes and jewelry;

The Visionary French

In Grandville's *Un Autre Monde*, sea plants, shells and corals assume bizarre, imaginatively unnatural forms [left]; and pipes and faucets come to life in a mechanical concert of a singer accompanied by horn and drum [above].

Gustave Moreau: *Hercules and the Hydra
of Lerne,* ca. 1876, 70¾ inches high
[Richard L. Feigen, Chicago; colorplate
Museum of Modern Art, New York].

Delilah, 12⅛ inches high, is one of many
roughly brushed sketches among the works
Moreau left to the State at his death.
They remain on view in his Paris house,
now the Musée Moreau. [Colorplate
Museum of Modern Art, New York].

Baudelaire is suggested both ways. His poetry is conspicuously and unprecedentedly rich in sonal, coloristic, imagistic and other correspondences; moreover, the bedecked lady—even Salomé is usually seen bearing a heavy load of decor, which the painter incessantly pictured—is unquestionably the sister of Baudelaire's perfect fatal lady:

La très-chère était nue, et, connaissant mon coeur,
Elle n'avait gardé que ses bijoux sonores,
Dont le riche attirail lui donnait l'air vainqueur
Qu'ont dans leurs jours heureux les esclaves des Mores.

Moreau's second principle, stasis, which he equated with the truly spiritual (somewhat in the manner of a detective evaluating the late nineteenth-century nude *tableau vivant*), is also a passion of Baudelaire:

Je suis belle, ô mortels! comme un rêve de pierre . . .
Je trône dans l'azur comme un sphinx incompris;
J'unis un coeur de neige à la blancheur des cygnes;
Je haïs le mouvement qui déplace les lignes,
Et jamais je ne pleure et jamais je ne ris.

The Visionary French

Though the esthetic is the same, the passion—and after all, Moreau is, compared to France's greatest modern poet, a lesser artist—is different. Was the connection with Baudelaire conscious? Certainly Baudelaire's willing acceptance, indeed, encouragement of the bejeweled and fatal woman would be unacceptable to Moreau, just as Baudelaire's feeling that "It is necessary to be modern" would have been anathema to the younger creator. We already know that Poe, whom Baudelaire translated, and who was his

favorite poet, was considered excessively morbid by Moreau. "I know it's the style these days to think otherwise," Moreau once remarked, "but don't forget that art ought to elevate, ennoble, moralize—yes, even moralize." Moreau once complained that "I have suffered too much in my life from the unjust and absurd opinion that I am too literary to be a painter." The suffering may have been unnecessary. The well-known tragedy of Moreau's literariness may have been less a result of being inspired by literature than of being inspired in the wrong way. The extent to which Moreau is old-fashioned has nothing to do with his literary interests, which if anything led him toward a certain fortunate modernization.

In Huysmans' *A Rebours* there is a passage in which the novelist's ultimate Symbolist-Decadent hero, des Esseintes, speaks of some new paintings he has purchased, by Moreau and Redon. Indeed, when Redon began to paint, Moreau was the only French painter of any significance whose images had primarily extra-earthly connections. Redon himself seems to have immediately launched a kind of art which remained beyond Moreau. In his remarkable journal, *A soi-même,* Redon made the following notation about Delacroix, whom he had always considered as one of his masters: "Since we are in the nineteenth century, he borrows the principal situations for his pictures from the poets of this century." Redon himself had a fervent, lifelong enthusiasm for the latest works of the Symbolists. It appears to have been implanted in the artist by his first real teacher, an enthusiast of new developments in both modern science and literature. While the painter was still in his 'teens, his friend Armand Clavaud "made me read Edgar Allan Poe and *Les Fleurs du Mal* the instant they were published . . . When Flaubert's first books came out he saw their future immediately and urged me to read them." Redon's own attitude toward literary painting was unequivocally enthusiastic. He wrote in a review in 1868: "This is not the moment to open the eyes of those who insist on restricting the painter's work to the reproduction of what he sees. Those who remain within these narrow limits commit themselves to an inferior goal. The old masters have proved that the artist, once he has established his own idiom, once he has taken from nature the necessary means of expression, is free, legitimately free, to borrow his subjects from history, from the poets, from his own imagination, from the thousand sources of his fantasy. That makes the superior artist: face to face with nature he is a painter, but alone in his studio he is a poet and a thinker."

Among Redon's first poems in painted form were versions of Delacroix; his first prints were executed under the direct tutelage of Bresdin, whom Redon often visited in southern France. Redon's first etching bears the notation, "pupil of Bresdin, 1865." He appears to have learned from Bresdin not only technique in the strictest sense, but also the technique of cultivating vision. "Do you see this chimney flue?" Bresdin is reported as asking. "What does it tell you? To me it tells a story. If you have the energy to observe it well and to understand it, then you will imagine the strangest and most bizarre subjects."

Redon's imagination soon began flourishing in the recommended directions. The most remarkable of the artist's earlier works are the series of lithographs he executed, beginning in 1878 with a group titled, appropriately enough, *Dans le Rêve.* The work is scattered throughout with reminiscences of both Moreau (whom Redon was eventually to reject as too scientific and "essentially worldly" an artist) and Bresdin (whom Redon admired throughout his life). The specific references are many—Moreau's image of the suspended head of St. John is echoed by numerous floating eyes and heads within this single work; Bresdin's more or less naturalistically landscaped backgrounds seem to be the theater for several of Redon's supernatural events. More important, the visionary method, involving the seeking of subject beyond painting, is theirs. A more direct plunge into literature was essayed in *A Edgar Poe* (1882). Here, above titles and quotations from the writer (some of which Redon, rather nervily, appears to have made up himself in a Poe-like style; Mallarmé is said to have admired their fine phrasing), the world of Poe was both alluded to and transcribed. Perhaps Redon's best-known print is here: titled *"L'Oeil, comme un ballon bizarre se dirige vers l'infini,"* it opens the series with a work simultaneously recalling Moreau's severed skulls, Grandville's *L'Oeillade* and the balloon-trip in Poe's *The Unparalleled Adventures of One Hans Pfaall,* as well as, perhaps, the astronomer Flammarion's recently published *Voyages en Ballon.* Scientific writings, evidently those of Darwin on evolution, as well as Grandville's improbable fusions of animal and plant characteristics, seem to have combined in *Les Origines* (1883). Redon dedicated no less than three separate cycles of lithographs to Gustave Flaubert, identifying them as illustra-

The Visionary French

Moreau: *The Suitors* [above] and detail of a young prince, struck down by Ulysses' arrow [right]. Ulysses stands inconspicuously at the rear in a doorway, as he takes his revenge on all those vying for his wife during his 20-year absence. The foreground is extravagantly strewn with his victims, and an apparition of Athena presides in a central burst of light [Musée Moreau, Paris].

tions relating to the *Temptation of St. Anthony* (a work which, ironically, Flaubert considered an extravagance and an indiscretion). Illustrations for an *Apocalypse of St. John*; *A Haunted House* by Bulwer-Lytton; a frontispiece for the Belgian poet Verhaeren's *Les Soirs*; and a projected series in connection with writings of DeQuincey (whose "technique for dreaming" Redon had come to admire) were also to follow. In 1890 Redon published his *Les Fleurs du Mal: Interprétations*. That it is far from the artist's strongest cycle is sadly true; and yet the project may have been redundant, since there was already so much Baudelaire in Redon's approach. ("I love that which has never been," Redon was to remark toward the end of his life.)

Redon's profound feeling for what the modern poets were accomplishing was intensified in the 1880s by increasing contacts with the young Symbolist group. Redon was almost 50 years old, when, to a critic who had composed an especially comprehending article on his work, he wrote: "Thank you. The help which you generously and with so much sympathy have brought me, dissipates much of my anguish and I feel myself nobler, now that I can continue to work for young spirits." Huysmans introduced Redon to Mallarmé, of whom he immediately became a close friend; from here on Redon's direct associations with other Symbolist writers multiplied. In his last years, Redon's art literally flowered—bouquets, often in connection with mysterious visages, are particularly frequent. Their richness of *correspondance* in themselves and with other arts supported the painter's position as a kind of poet's hero. Even the new school of Symbolist painters, the Nabis, acknowledged the genius of Redon and Gauguin practically alone among contemporary painters.

In 1886 (the year of the Verhaeren frontispiece) Redon was invited to exhibit with the rising group of Belgian avant-garde artists, *Les Vingt.* He accepted this homage "with a feeling of joy—a sweet reward." That visionary art, especially when related to literary sources, had not triumphed is shown by the fact that James Ensor, who participated with Redon in the 1886 exhibition, had one of his most important drawings rejected the

The Visionary French

James Ensor: *Intrigue,* 1890, 35⅜ inches high [detail, left; Royal Museum of Fine Arts, Antwerp].

Ensor: *Tribulations of St. Anthony,* 1887, 46⅜ inches high [right, and detail, below; Modern Museum, New York].

following year: *Hail Jesus, the King of the Jews.* This artist had many of the same interests in literature as Redon and his predecessors. Like Bresdin, he, too, imagined skeletons intent on suspiciously earthly activities (playing billiards, fighting for food, trying to warm themselves at a stove), as if earth itself were some kind of intolerable hell. The Dance of Death and other medieval legends not only inspired a good many of Ensor's paintings, but much of his graphic work—the *Seven Deadly Sins* drawings, the series of savage etchings picturing professionals abusing their professions: *The Dangerous Cooks, The Bad Doctors, The Infamous Vivisectors.* By the 1890 exhibition (where Redon exhibited, and attended side by side with Mallarmé), Ensor had an entire series of paintings rejected, including one of his best works, *Masks Confronting Death.* Poe had been preoccupied by masks in his stories; Ensor read Poe with pleasure and illustrated one of his tales in his famous etching (later a painting) *The Vengeance of Hop-Frog.* Baudelaire had devoted a series of bitter, satirical epigrams (*Amoenitates Belgicae*) to what he considered the bourgeois spirit of Belgium; now the artists (who eventually excluded Ensor from their circle) were again proving it. The paintings which thematically succeeded *Hail Jesus* were among Ensor's greatest: among them the mural-size *Entry of Christ into Brussels.*

It was appropriate that the first monograph on the most astonishingly intense of all nineteenth-century visionaries (astonishing for an intensity which was to burn out around 1900, although Ensor lived until the middle of the twentieth century) should have been written by the Belgian Symbolist, Emile Verhaeren. Still, Ensor's connection with the future of modern literature may have been even firmer: for both the fat, fraudulent royal figure in the 1889 etching, *Belgium in the Twentieth Century,* and the fat and navel-contemplating figures on the beach in *White and Red Clowns Tumbling* (1890) are unmistakably Ubu-esque. Alfred Jarry's monstrous bourgeois king has more than a little in common with James Ensor's, and except for the fact that Jarry illustrated his own text so effectively, it is regrettable that Ensor himself never illustrated an edition of *Ubu Roi* (first published in 1896). As it was, Redon worked with greater effectiveness, later, than did Ensor.

It is fitting that Redon should have lived and worked effectively until 1916—the same year that Symbolism's successor-movement was initiated. In 1916 Dada was born, in Switzerland, and Surrealism—with its enthusiasm for all extra-painterly and particularly literary analogies—was not far behind. The visionary had become an accepted element in vanguard style.

The Visionary French

In Hugo's pen and wash sketch titled *My Destiny,* the author of *Les Travailleurs de la mer* romantically symbolizes his political exile [Victor Hugo Museum, Paris].

Rodolphe Bresdin's *Comedy of Death,* the famous print which inspired Gautier's poem of the same name, which he dedicated to the artist.

III

The Joys and Enigmas of a Strange Hour

By John Ashbery

Few people today have heard of Max Klinger (born 1857 in Leipzig; died 1920 at Gross-jena, near Naumburg), and these few would be even fewer if Giorgio de Chirico had not admired him to the point of writing an admiring article on his work, published in the review *Il Convegno* in 1920. Klinger thus joined Raphael, Courbet and Böcklin in the bizarre cenacle of artists to whom Chirico has paid written homage. Metaphysics makes strange bedfellows.

Reading Chirico on Klinger is like listening to a brilliant defense attorney who is fully aware of his power of moving the most hard-hearted jury to tears. "What is this romanticism of modern life?"[1] he asks. "It is the breath of yearning that flows over the capitals of cities, over the geometry of suburban factories, over the apartment houses that rise like cement or stone cubes, over the sea of houses and buildings, compressing within their hard flanks the sorrows and hopes of insipid daily life. It is the pretentious private residence in the breathless torpor of a springtime morning or the moonlit calm of a summer night, with all the shutters closed behind the garden trees and the wrought-iron gates. It is the nostalgia of railroad stations, of arrivals and departures, the anxiety of seaports

Scene [right], 10⅛ inches high, the first in a series of ten etchings entitled *A Glove* (1881) by the German artist Max Klinger. The sequence, a kind of novel in pictures, recounts the fantastic peregrinations of a lost glove. The scene shown here was an actual roller-skating rink in Berlin. At far left, Klinger (in striped trousers) with his friend Prell, watches the arrival of a beautiful Brazilian girl. In *Action* [left], 11¾ inches high, the second episode of the series, Klinger retrieves the girl's glove and thus precipitates a series of bizarre events. [All reproductions from prints in the Museum of Modern Art, New York].

where ships, their hawsers loosened, sail into the black waters of the night, their lights aglitter as in cities on a holiday." Elsewhere in the essay he says, "The pictorial question did not matter, because his entire creation was based on the enormous possibilities of his exceptional mind—the mind of a poet, philosopher, observer, dreamer and psychologist." Which reminds one of Chirico's definition of art in his early essay, *Meditations of a Painter:* "A truly immortal work of art can only be born through revelation. Schopenhauer has, perhaps, best defined and also (why not) explained such a moment when in *Parerga and Paralipomena* he says, 'To have original, extraordinary, and perhaps even immortal ideas, one has but to isolate oneself from the world for a few moments so completely that the most commonplace happenings appear to be new and unfamiliar, and in this way reveal their true essence.' If, instead of the birth of *original, extraordinary, immortal* ideas, you imagine the birth of a work of art (painting or sculpture) in an artist's mind, you will have the principle of revelation in painting."

"The pictorial question did not matter . . ." Despite the nineteenth-century sound of "principle of revelation," Klinger is one of those artists who transcend the restrictions of the pictorial question and therefore of criticism. Appearances to the contrary, he is a colleague of such artists as Duchamp, Mondrian or Chirico himself. In each of these cases, the "meaning" of art is offstage—either (as with Chirico and Klinger) buried so deep inside the work that no one can find it; or (as with Mondrian) somehow adjacent to the work but out of sight; or (as with Duchamp) just absent. Thus, if we accept Klinger at all as an artist (and probably, in the absence of any case for the prosecution, we shall have to admit Chirico's virtuoso defense), we must forget about "the pictorial question" and accept both the academic virtues for which he was admired in his day, and also the "faults" of drawing and composition for which he was sometimes scolded by his contemporaries (for example, the stern Elizabeth Luther Carey of the *New York Times,* who was perhaps not so far wrong in her estimate of Klinger: "We may say that his drawing is sometimes poor, his imagination clumsy, his treatment of a subject coarse, but . . . out of his figures looks the spirit of life, more often defiant than noble, more often capricious than beautiful, but not to be mistaken.")

Although Klinger was a painter and a sculptor (his realistic, polychrome statues of nudes approach the ultimate in creepiness), what little reputation he has today rests on his engravings, especially the series called *A Glove* (so titled in its first and third editions; the second edition was entitled *Paraphrase on the Finding of a Glove.*) While individual engravings and another sequence called *Fantasy on Brahms* are also notable, *A Glove* is the most prodigal of what Chirico, in the title of one of his paintings, calls "the joys and enigmas of a strange hour."

Although the *Glove's* scenario was given its due Germanic explication by contemporary critics, it defies rational analysis. The last picture, which was seen as a kind of happy ending to the glove's peregrinations, is particularly ambiguous and leaves the whole meaning of the series in doubt. The story is a parable of loss about a trivial lost article, like the lost keys in *Bluebeard* and in *Alice,* like Desdemona's missing handkerchief, or like the philosopher's spectacles in Klinger's own *Fantasy on Brahms,* which have slid out of their proprietor's reach just as he was nearing the summit of a kind of Matterhorn. There are overtones of erotic symbolism and fetishism in the glove and the phalloid monster who abducts it, heightened for a modern viewer by the Krafft-Ebing period costumes and décors (the engravings appeared in 1881, and the drawings were apparently finished in 1878).

Scene, the first plate in the series, seems at first to be a perfectly straightforward vignette of a group of people standing around in a Berlin roller-skating rink; the two at extreme left have been identified as portraits of Klinger (in striped trousers) and his friend Prell. But as one continues to look at the picture it becomes curiouser and curiouser. Several of the figures are looking out toward the viewer at a new arrival whom we cannot see, no doubt the owner of the glove whom we shall glimpse in the next plate. Her invisible presence already sets up a current of uneasiness. In addition, to quote the critic Paul Kuhn, "the figures standing around and greeting each other are lifeless, as in a fashion plate." All, that is, except the little girl who has just taken a spill. Her arrested motion makes us realize that what we are looking at is actually a kind of high-speed snapshot, in spite of the relaxed, lounging poses of the other figures.

Plate II, *Action,* presents the crucial, irrevocable moment of the drama. Everything contributes to give the scene that strangely immortal look that our surroundings take on during a moment of crisis: the arbitrary framing of the hero in the outline of the distant

The Joys and Enigmas
of a Strange Hour

In *Desires* (III; 12½ inches high), the
hero is watched from afar by the glove's
owner. The trees and the outline of the
forest have taken on a glove-like look.

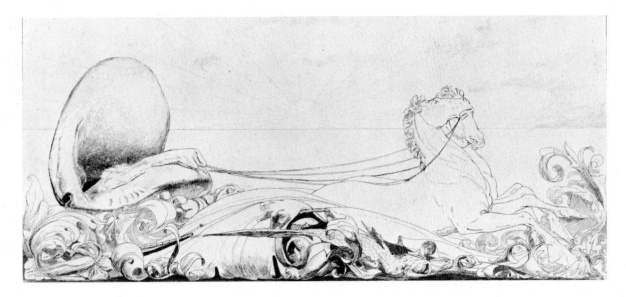

In *Triumph* (V; 5⅝ inches high), the glove drives a chariot across the sea.

The Joys and Enigmas of a Strange Hour

Wearing the hat he dropped in Plate II, the hero in *Rescue* (IV; 9⅜ inches high), tries to retrieve the drowning glove.

terrace (a device also used by such masters of the bizarre as Carpaccio and Balthus); the strange, phallic dome of the pergola; the stiffly swaying postures of the background figures including the mysterious lady herself: in this, our only close look at her, we see only her back. (Some critics call her "the Brazilian," and Kuhn identifies her with an actual Brazilian girl whose graceful roller-skating was for a time the talk of Berlin).

With the fatal purloining of the glove begin the hero's dream misadventures. In each of the succeeding plates the glove appears as in a puzzle; sometimes it is tiny and almost invisible; sometimes it swells to monstrous proportions as though to call attention to the protagonist's complex sin: at once a theft, a transgression of sexual taboos, and the always-fatal worship of an image rather than the reality it symbolizes—literally, in this case, the container instead of the thing contained. In *Dreams* (III), the hero is safe in bed with his trophy before him on the coverlet, but he seems to be lost in anguished dreams. There are other signs that already all is not well: a young woman, the Brazilian no doubt, is watching him from a distance; and nature (the slender trees, the forest on the hillside) has begun to take on disquieting resemblances to the object of his monomania. (Furniture in a landscape, such as we see here, is a theme that frequently occurs in Chirico's paintings of the 1920s, such as the circa 1927 *Furniture in the Valley*; and in his prose.)

The hero is next seen (in *Rescue*) in a small boat, trying to fish the glove out of a

Homage (VI; 6¼ inches high). The glove accepts a gift of roses from the sea.

In *Anguish* (VII; 5⅝ inches high), aquatic monsters plague the dreamer.

The Joys and Enigmas of a Strange Hour

billowy sea. It is worth noting that he is now wearing his hat, which he dropped the moment he picked up the glove, although it seems hardly appropriate to his present nautical role. In *Triumph* the glove is riding a conch-shell chariot drawn by two coursers through a tide of flowers; it grips the reins with a force that is in utter contrast with its helpless state in *Rescue*. This plate marks the first appearance of one of the crocodile-like creatures who seem to be the glove's custodians. In *Homage* we find that the glove lies on a kind of altar at the edge of the sea and seems to be accepting offerings from the waves, which are strewn with roses.

Next, in *Anguish*, the most spectacular plate of the series, the sea invades the hero's bedroom in a Freudian nightmare awash with sexual symbols, such as the candle, the moon, the dugs of the witches, and the white, feminine hands that are reaching out for the glove, which has become monstrous and dominates the other objects in the room. One recalls Auden's "The mouse you banished yesterday/Is an enraged rhinoceros today."

Somehow the hero again retrieves his quarry, for in the next plate, *Peace*, he has placed it on a table in a little sanctuary closed off by a curtain of gloves, perhaps so that it will

A reptilian glovenapper parts a curtain of gloves in *Peace* (VIII; 5⅝ inches high).

In *Abduction* (IX; 4¾ inches high), the monster makes off with his prey.

feel at home. But such subterfuges, as we know from Proust's *The Captive*, never succeed. The crocodile is already parting the curtain with its snout, and in *Abduction*, the penultimate picture, it flies off with it into the night, as the hero's arms grasp futilely through the panes of a broken window. (How the crocodile managed to get through one of the holes in the window is one of the many enigmas of the series.)

In the last plate, *Amor*, the glove is once more in a sanctuary, watched over by a smirking cupid. But it is impossible to say whether this sanctuary is the hero's night table, as some writers (including Chirico) have supposed. It is more likely something in the nature of Pandora's box, a repository for archetypal erotic trifles, where the glove will remain until it is next needed to trouble the sleep of mortals. But one cannot say for sure. One of the properties of the metaphysical, of "art by revelation," is to elude the very definitions it proposes. The secret of such art is, like the glove, something inviolable, despite the hazards which surround it and are its natural element.

[1]This and other quotations from Chirico are from James Thrall Soby's *Giorgio de Chirico,* Museum of Modern Art, New York, 1955.

The glove is guarded by a cupid in *Amor,* the last etching (5⅝ inches high).

54

IV

The Canticles of Hieronymus Bosch

By Mario Praz

Author

Mario Praz holds the Chair of English
Literature at the University of Rome. He
is the author of the influential study,
The Romantic Agony, and monographs on
Empire style furniture, the 19th-century
novel, the fantastic sculptures at
Bomarzo, the wood carvings by Pianta,
and many other volumes. This essay was
translated into English by the author.

An irrepressible taste for the
bizarre transmutes reality in
Bosch's sheet of *Beggars and Rogues,*
pen and ink, 11⅛ inches high
[Albertina, Vienna]. Related
in style and subject to his early
work, these are undoubtedly studies
for some lost painting.

The last decade has seen an extraordinary reawakening of interest in bizarre and unusual
art. In France and Italy especially this revival has prompted a number of books on the
subject[1] which, in a century as fond of categories and genres as the eighteenth, would
have culminated in a *Philosophical Enquiry* like Burke's. But the territory is so vast, and
our faith in definitions so weak, that it is no wonder that most of the books in question
are little more than astonishing accumulations of curios. Roger Caillois, however, has
tried to limit the fantastic to its less obvious manifestations. Thus he would give all the
"ostentatious deviltries" and "systematic hybridizations" of Bosch for his "secretly strange"
Marriage at Cana. Actually the eccentric defies definitions by the very fact of its being
eccentric. The deliberately eccentric is as valid as the stealthily eccentric. The bizarre is
no less individual than humor. It is easier to say what it is not than what it is. Bosch is
an eccentric—and so is Goya. Then there are a number of eccentrics who impress us as
such, but who would be surprised to see themselves so classified. Did the compilers of
books of emblems—moral, political, alchemical—see themselves as eccentric, even though
Caillois includes them in his short list? Did Kircher consider himself one? Just as we
would hardly classify the Renaissance masters of *sacre conversazioni* as landscape painters
because of the occasional landscapes in their backgrounds, so we may well hesitate to call
those artists bizarre who surprise us by some unexpected quaintness, some uncanny detail
in an otherwise straightforward composition. This occasional strangeness may have various
causes: one is the fact that the artists refer to symbols and allegories which have become
unfamiliar and therefore strike us as odd (e.g. the illustrators of emblem books); another
cause is an obsession which betrays itself in a particular insistence on certain details (as
in the fetishism of Fuseli). Then there is the deliberate distortion of the carvers of Classical gems who invented what Pliny the Elder called *grylli*; the no less weird fantasy of
Gothic sculptors—and the "systematic hybridizations" of Hieronymus Bosch.

It is rather surprising that André Breton, in the last edition of his *Le Surréalisme et la
Peinture,*[2] does not even mention Hieronymus Bosch, whom painters of that tendency
have always seen as a forerunner. Even if they had named him their father, they would
not have said enough, nor would they have said the right thing. If a modest corollary may
gratify an eminent theorem with the name of forerunner, if a servile and self-conscious
follower[3] may, in an act of courteous condescension, admit having been anticipated by
the author from whom he derives, then Hieronymus Bosch may rightly be termed the
first spark of that bonfire, Salvador Dali. But in fact we have only to compare the compo-
sitions of Dali with the central figure of the Hell section of the *Garden of Delights* (at
the Escorial, where it goes under the name of *Las Lujurias*), to become aware that Bosch
had not only said everything there was to say, but also infinitely more.

In the center of a grim, blazing landscape of Hell, teeming with life, a white monster,
crouching immodestly, presents us a rump formed by a colossal egg, to which, by means
of pliant human joints, are fitted hollow trunks of dead trees whose sharp bare branches

pierce the gigantic shell. At one end hovers a disc surmounted by a bagpipe, and under this hat you see a man's face,[4] pale and uncanny in its utter impropriety, whose eyes seem to wink at his posterior—the gaping egg-shell—which he thrusts out at us. Inside there is the Bagpipe Inn (the sign is painted on a banner fixed to one of the dead branches), where a witch, under the sulphurous gaze of an owl, pours from a cask to sinners seated round a table in the half-light, while another tiny man leans desolately musing on the jagged brim of the shell (some maintain that this is the painter himself, oppressed by the weight of his nightmare). The disc topping the head is used as a platform by horned and billed devils and witches who are leading by the hand other diminutive sinners, stark naked. More ghostlike figures are climbing a ladder leaning against the broken shell: a hooded one has a wooden pin in place of a tail, and a shivering naked one shrugs his shoulders as though on the point of diving into icy water, pushed by a devil with a raven's head, butterfly wings and the sheathed legs of a beetle. Pages of elaborate descriptions would not suffice to give an idea of the swarming composition: "fantastical and capricious inventions that it would be tiresome to describe one by one," as Vasari said. Fantastical and capricious we may grant, but if they were completely arbitrary they would not grip us and frighten us. Even before the moderns discovered a kind of forerunner of Freud in Bosch, Fray José de Siguença, in the *Tercera parte de la Historia de la Orden de San Geronimo,* published in Madrid in 1605, wrote: "The difference there is, in my opinion, between the paintings of this man and those of the others, lies in this: that the others usually try to paint men as they appear on the outside, but this one alone has dared to paint them as they are inside."

At the borderline of the Middle Ages, when the Gothic was blazing out in delicate flames whose flamboyant patterns had long been smoldering in the hothouses of the royal courts, and were leaving traces even on the Italian Renaissance (serpentine graces of Boticelli, rapturous deliquescences of Filippino Lippi, Crivelli's jewelries and trimmings), centuries of pious meditations on the wounds of Christ and the torments of hell, of allegories of vices and passions, of other-worldly visions and imagined interior vistas, picture-books of the beginnings of psychology, all flared up in a supreme bonfire before Reason pushed the Gog and Magog of the subconscious beyond the ramparts of its classical wall. What a Bonvesin da Riva had crudely depicted, what Dante had tried to represent in his powerful verse: twinings and metamorphoses of men and snakes, specters cloven from chin to loins, holding their severed heads like lanterns, dragons tattooed with knots, wheels having the faces of honest men, chariots changing into hydras with horned ox-like heads—all this population of ghosts into which the medieval man, in a kind of day-dream, concretized his inner world, all this Hieronymus Bosch painted with a power of hallucination such as no one of the serene artists of Italy could ever have equaled. How cold and contrived Giovanni Bellini's allegories appear to us—where monsters are clusters of reasoned-out, not felt, attributes—compared to Bosch's visions! When an Italian artist tried to imitate Bosch's monsters, he felt obliged to place the figure of a man asleep in the center of the picture, as though to ward off a possible accusation of preposterousness with the anticlimax: "It is just a dream!"[5]

The medieval taste for the fantastic was further developed in Bosch by the wide-spread vogue for talismans from archaic and classical cultures, with their grotesque figures. After the sack of Constantinople by the Crusaders in 1204, its treasures were scattered throughout the West; one may deplore that senseless barbarity of Christians against Christians, but just as the catastrophe of Vesuvius, by burying Pompeii and Herculaneum, allowed antiquity to survive almost intact and resulted in a Neo-Classical revival centuries later, so the loot of Constantinople was indirectly responsible for the animal-crested medieval helmets inspired by classic gems, as well as for the preposterous shapes of Bosch's monsters, drawn from ancient coins, Assyrian cylinders and Hellenistic intaglios: we find in those ancient seals the stork-shaped ship as well as the fish-shaped one of the Lisbon *Temptation of St. Anthony.*[6] The taste for the bizarre was also stimulated by remoter hybridizations—influences from the Far East which reached Europe in the course of the thirteenth century. Bosch's arborescent devils and anthropomorphous mountains and rocks are Chinese contributions.

The quintessence of the medieval imagination had accumulated to such a degree in this belated, provincial artist, that to define him as "belated" would be no less improper than to define Shakespeare as a belated follower of the medieval stage: such deeper ventures in style and outlook transcend time. The medieval world reaches a supreme ex-

The Canticles of Hieronymus Bosch

Central panel and detail of Bosch's *Temptation of St. Anthony* [National Museum, Lisbon]. Among scenes depicted on the ruined tower that serves as sanctuary for the Saint are seen: Moses Receiving the Tablets of the Law, the Worship of the Golden Calf and a sacrificial offering of a swan to an animal deity, the latter two as prefigurations of medieval heresies.

pression in Bosch: with its scaffolds, its limb-breaking wheels, its fires, its armed bands perpetually threatening the countryside—we may find that Bosch's Middle Ages bear a strong resemblance to what Marcel Schwob imagined they were like. We should notice, however, not so much the picturesque grimness of a vanished age as a universal landscape of the soul. Some Latin verse of the end of the sixteenth century, written under the effigy of Hieronymus Bosch, ran:

Quid sibi vult, Hieronyme Boschi,
Ille oculus tuus attonitus? quid
Pallor in ore? velut lemures si
Spectra Erebi volitantia coram
Aspiceres?

[O, Hieronymus Bosch, what is the meaning of/that terrified eye of yours? What means/ the pallor of your face? As if you were/seeing ghosts, specters of Hell shifting/before you?[7]].

We feel almost tempted to introduce an emendation into this text, and to read, instead of *Erebi, cerebri.* Thus Bosch would immediately appear as a forerunner of Freud. This is less paradoxical than it seems, nor is the psychoanalytical interpretation of Bosch's paintings which Charles de Tolnay has attempted in his monograph entirely arbitrary,[8] since it appears that Bosch had recourse to dreams and to books explaining them for his pictorial ideas, just as Freud based his psychoanalytical theories on them, and the material of dreams is as proper to one epoch as to another: dreams are eternal shapes, which repeat themselves like the visions of the mystics. Let us remember what Charles Lamb wrote (in "Witches, and Other Night-Fears" in the *Essays of Elia*) about a child who, brought up in the most rigorous exclusion from every taint of superstition, found in his own "thick-coming fancies" all that world of fear, from which he had been so scrupulously excluded: "Gorgons, and Hydras, and Chimeras—dire stories of Celaeno and the Harpies—may reproduce themselves in the brain of superstition—but they were there before. They are transcripts, types—the archetypes are in us, and eternal. How else should the recital of that, which we know in a waking sense to be false, come to affect us at all?"

For de Tolnay, Bosch's symbols, taken from simple elements belonging to all the spheres of nature, and from the homeliest objects, are at the mercy of a perpetual metamorphosis; but the more we are astonished by the fantastic aspect they assume, the closer they bring us to reality; under the guise of a play of pure imagination, they are precise embodiments of vice. (This, by the way, suggests a definition of Surrealism.) So in the lists of horrible ingredients of the witches' cauldron in *Macbeth,* we almost see a spectral projection of the crimes of the usurper.

How does Hieronymus Bosch contrive his obsessive effects? His capital triptychs, the Lisbon *Temptation of St. Anthony,* the Escorial *Garden of Delights,* give us an idea of his resources. First of all, he does away with any allusion to real space. His bands of ghosts approach us as if on the crests of waves. The landscape is not seen in depth, but almost as a bird's-eye view. In the central portion of the *Garden of Delights,* it spreads upwards and swarms with creatures, like the exuberant marginal decoration of an illuminated manuscript. A tapestry, a hanging mirage, a painted veil confronts us. The sense of unreality is enhanced by the fact that certain objects are shown in disparate scales: a head is placed on the ground like the colossal helmet Horace Walpole was going to introduce into his castle of Otranto in order to cause terror; a giant oyster; a formidable knife; a pair of ears; an owl's head; a harp; a hurdy-gurdy—all loom hugely in the swarm of demons, animals and naked men, upsetting all sense of proportion, breaking the vision into two layers, as in the overlapping of dreams, or in one of those Victorian screens made of pasted odds and ends. See for instance the juxtaposition of birds and humans in a section of the *Garden of Delights*: those woodpeckers, kingfishers, hoopoes and drakes, which would have looked pretty on the margin of an illuminated page, here, mixed as they are with men half their size, acquire a sinister, hallucinatory quality. A naked man holds a strawberry as big as his chest. And look at those monstrous castles in the upper part of the painting, which partake of the nature of fruits, of beetles, of minerals, of crustaceans, hirsute with antennae, half-moons, lobsters' claws and coral branches, swelling like sailing ships, threatening as cannonballs.

The scene is glimpsed as through a medium more magical than air, almost in an aquarium light. The tints are soft, they charm us with delicate hues, even if they clothe

The Canticles of
Hieronymus Bosch

Detail from the central panel of the *Temptation of St. Anthony* [National Museum, Lisbon]. A demon with a tonsured pig head is celebrating a black mass; he is attended by two acolytes, one with an inverted funnel on his head, symbolizing human folly; the other carrying a nest with egg, symbol of alchemical processes. All colorplates in this article were specially photographed for a new edition of Charles de Tolnay's *Hieronymus Bosch,* published by Reynal & Company, New York.

world (one of the most widespread themes of this category of the bizarre, the hare and the hunter reversing their positions, is found in the Hell section of the *Garden of Delights*), at the service of a sect of heretics to which he belonged himself? And when we think of it, to what other use could a triptych like the *Garden of Delights* be put? Although the creation of Adam and Eve appears in one wing (but why has the Creator the aspect of a youthful Christ?), and a representation of Hell in the other one, the central panel contains a crowd of naked human beings who are certainly not gathered for a Last Judgment; and if we remember the usual depictions of this subject and of the joys of Paradise by Fra Angelico, we immediately become aware that Bosch's scene is of another kind altogether. Would such a triptych be fit for the altar of an "average" Christian church?

Hence the theory of Wilhelm Fraenger,[10] which offers an explanation of this mystery: Bosch's bizarre vision was systematic because it had been inspired by the master of one of the sects of the movement of the Free Spirit, and the portrait of this patron would be the person, the only one to be dressed, in the right corner of the central panel, appearing behind a naked woman resting her head on her left arm, a kind of sibyl represented as the keeper of a secret wisdom by the seal on her lips, and a new Eve by the apple she holds in her right hand; they both emerge from a Pythagorean cavern against whose opening is tilted the crystal slab which formerly closed it, a slab dotted with five disks; the center of each disk is marked: four of them correspond to arterial points of the woman's body, namely the wrist of her right hand, the arteries of the elbows, and the one of the neck; the fifth lies on one of her breasts.

I have given this minute description because it is typical of Fraenger's long analysis of the painting, each detail being interpreted symbolically in the light of theological, philosophical and alchemical ideas, partly current in Bosch's time, partly contained in later texts (Novalis, Johann Jakob Bachofen); and all these ideas concur to establish that syncretism between Christian religion and pagan philosophy which characterized Florentine Neo-Platonism. As for the movement of the Free Spirit, thanks to the studies of Romana Guarnieri,[11] we know more about it now than when Fraenger wrote his book.

To call it a movement of piety which here and there degenerated into impiousness is inadequate; we are confronted with an epidemic of a type at times benign, but more frequently malignant, which expresses itself in words which in the mouth of some (the orthodox believers) mean one thing, and in that of others (the heretics) another. St. Bernard said: "The freed spirit becomes one with God." Doctrines of Oriental theology about *deificatio* were transmitted chiefly through the Catharists and found favor with the followers of Gioacchino da Fiore, with the Speronists, the Amalricians and others. How does this process of reaching a state similar to that of the Creator relate to the followers of the movement of the Free Spirit? A process, by the way, that has points of contact with certain trends of Arab mysticism, either orthodox or heterodox (the Sufis), which in its turn seems to have assimilated Indian elements.

The great Flemish mystic Ruusbroec described the process with a wealth of details and a psychological and theological lucidity. According to him, those heretics "are lost in the empty and blind simplicity of their own essence, and mean to be blessed within the bare limits of their own nature. They are so simple and to such an extent united without an intermediary to the bare essence of their soul and to the essential presence of God in them, that they do not feel any zeal or inclination towards God, either internally or externally, because on the summit where they lie collected they experience nothing else but the simplicity of their essence, which hangs in the essence of God; and thus they assume God to be such absolute simplicity, in which they enjoy a natural calm, and therefore they take themselves to be God, in the bottom of their own simplicity. They lack real faith, hope and charity, and meanwhile, in the empty and naked state they experience and possess, they claim to have neither knowledge nor love, and to be exonerated from every virtue. As a consequence of all this they try to live without conscience, whatever evil they may do, utterly neglecting the sacraments, virtues and observances of the Holy Church, of which they think they have no further need, esteeming themselves above all these things which are fit for imperfect men. . . . The highest degree of sanctity lies for them in following their own natural instinct in everything and unrestrainedly, so as to be able to remain inwardly idle, with their spirit prone to evil, and to indulge outwardly any impulse, thus satisfying the desires of the body, pleasing their flesh, and quickly eluding their imagination, so as to come back freely to the naked idleness of the spirit." Thus

The Canticles of Hieronymus Bosch

The Hell panel of *The Garden of Delights* triptych, consistent with the ideas of the Brethren of the Free Spirit, depicts the diabolic perversions of men not initiated to the doctrines of the new Adam: below the immodestly crouching white monster of Egoism are depicted the Musicians', Monks', Gamblers' and other hells.

wrote Ruusbroec towards the end of the fourteenth century, hinting in the last sentences at the excesses which ensued from those principles.

The Free Spirit movement has a double face, devout and infernal, highly spiritual and perversely licentious, and the two aspects pass one into the other by imperceptible degrees. The chief text, the *Miroir des simples âmes* by Marguerite Porete (born in Hainaut about 1250), unknown to Fraenger, deserves to rank among the masterpieces of the literature of mysticism. She was a heretical St. Catherine of Siena or St. Catherine of Genoa or St. Teresa, with her face covered by a black veil (like the bust of Marin Faliero, the traitor doge of Venice), because this nun was warned, tried and, finally, having not submitted, sentenced to the stake; she suffered her punishment (or martyrdom) on the Place de Grève, Paris, June 1, 1310.

What does Marguerite's *Miroir* say? The soul is saved through faith only, without works. She has neither comfort nor affection nor hope in any creature created by God, neither in heaven nor on earth, but only in God's goodness. The soul does not beg nor ask anything from any creature, she is the phoenix, which is alone, because she is alone in love, and is satisfied with herself; she has neither shame nor honor, neither leisure nor discomfort, neither love nor hate, neither hell nor paradise. She has everything and nothing; she knows everything and knows nothing; she wants everything and she wants nothing. And why should such a soul scruple to take what she needs of the four elements, as from the brightness of the sky, the heat of fire, the freshness of water, and the earth which sustains us? Such Souls make use of all things made and created, which are needed by nature; they are accustomed to understand much and to forget everything, through their lover's subtlety. "I am God," says Love, "because Love is God, and God is Love, and this Soul is God by love's condition, and I am God by divine nature, and this Soul is God through love's right." God has sanctified his name in her and the divine Trinity dwells in her. She drinks the beverage which no one else drinks, but the Trinity. And the soul, annihilated in God, is drunk with it, surpassingly drunk, more drunk than anybody ever was who drank or will drink. She is the eagle, she flies with the seraph's wings, she is the fire of love herself and she finds God in everything, and she is excused of everything because God is her will. Like wax sealed by God, she rests in peace. Like a mountain which is above the winds. She has taken leave of the virtues which are only anxiety and toil, she has crossed the sea in order to suck the marrow of the lofty cedar. Martha is worried, Mary has peace. She has gone beyond the sword's point, killing the body's delights and quenching the wishes of the spirit.

Accents like these call to mind Jacopone da Todi, who—a remarkable coincidence— walked naked in the streets like certain brothers of the Free Spirit (Aegidius Cantor, among others). Pages of Hadewych (the most mysterious mystical poetess of the Middle Ages), Eckhart, Jacopone, take on a new aspect if seen in the light of the texts of the Free Spirit which date chiefly from 1270-1310. This Free Spirit would be nothing else but the *nova filosofia* which, in Jacopone's words, *gli utri vecchi ha dissipato* (the new philosophy has burst the old wineskins).

St. Clare warned the Franciscan Fra Giovannuccio da Bevagna: *"Cave, cave frater, quia tu credis stare in alto, sed caveas de descensu et quomodo descendes."* [Beware, beware, brother; you think you are standing on high, yet beware of the descent and whither you will descend.⁷]

In a detailed chronicle of the movement of the Free Spirit from its origins to the sixteenth century, Romana Guarnieri reveals a pageant that would almost outweigh Flaubert's survey of heresies in his *Temptation of St. Anthony*: beguines of Silesia who, once they had become perfect through abstinence and flagellation, could gratify their appetites as they wished in order to recover what they had lost; the Mothers Superior of Schweidnitz who wore precious linen under their rags; Fra Dolcino who held copulation an act of the Holy Spirit; the naked dances (the so-called Paradises); the ritual orgies presided over by a couple who called themselves Jesus and Mary. Notwithstanding its aberrations, the movements of the Free Spirit should be judged not "a strangeness or foolishness of the soul" (to use the words with which Schopenhauer concluded his study of the points on which Western and Eastern mystics were in agreement), "but rather an essential side of human nature, which rarely shows itself owing to its excellence."

Actually the return to the Adamic state of innocence, which is the aspect of the movement of the Free Spirit that Fraenger sees represented in the central panel of the *Garden of Delights,* is a trait common also to D.H. Lawrence's creed: also in the triptych we find,

The Canticles of Hieronymus Bosch

The central panel of Bosch's triptych of *The Hay-Wain*, ca. 1510, 52 inches high [Prado, Madrid], is a satirical attack on the greed and hypocrisy of the Church and Empire. Conceived as a triumphal procession, the hay wagon—symbol of vanity—moves toward the right, to the Hell panel of the triptych.

according to Fraenger, a wreathed phallus, just as in an episode of *Lady Chatterley's Lover*. For the German critic, the Hell panel represents the damnation of the non-initiates, the central panel shows voluptuousness as not sinful, but rather as a return to the innocence of Paradise. In the portion of the central panel bordering Hell there are still hesitating souls, whereas others, having been initiated, are admitted through a gate; in the upper portion there is a triumphal cavalcade of naked youths round the pond of Life's water; in the lower part a dying man receives the Eucharist of euthanasia, and life and death join in a perennial cycle symbolized by the figures standing on their hands. The cavalcade of youths symbolizes mastery over the instincts; there are recurring symbols of the egg, the butterfly, the fish, this last being a supreme symbol of Christ (*ichthus*); and giant birds which are emblems of the instinct of reproduction, life-carriers; among the human figures the heads of the novices have no ornament, whereas those of the initiates have a mark of distinction such as a leaf, a flower or a fruit. The central panel is meant to celebrate a chaste, primitive love, but nevertheless it breathes an air of ambiguous voluptuousness, so much so that it has been liable to a quite opposite interpretation.

This negative interpretation would be the true one, if Bosch, as Castelli[12] and Jacques Combe[13] maintain, had been connected with a congregation emanating from the father of the *Devotio Moderna,* Geert Groot (died 1384), who fought the followers of the doctrine of the Free Spirit and other "perverted" mystics.[14] Combe writes: "Why should we try to find in Bosch's painting a paradise preached by a doctrine of purified sensuality (Fraenger), or to be identified with a kind of nirvana to which souls would be admitted after purgatory, according to Wertheim-Aymès' suggestion?[15] It does not seem to us that these interpretations disprove the traditional one (the picture has been called *La Lujuria* or *El cuadro del madrono* ever since the end of the sixteenth century); in our opinion between the earthly paradise (already threatened by temptation) and hell (full of allusions to the defeats of the soul) one may see a representation of the false kind of life to which the tempter persuades men. So the painting would be the conclusion of an idea which had already found momentous expression in the *Hay-Wain* and the Lisbon *St. Anthony.*"[16]

There is no doubt that the central panel of the *Hay-Wain* is a satire of the Church and the monastic orders and their vices (greed, gluttony, etc.), but the hieroglyph of the central panel of the *Garden of Delights* may show aspects which to us look perverse, but which never appear as caricatures. The recurring theme is, as Fraenger has emphasized, the highest form of love, the glorification of love and life. And while many of the allusions pointed out by Fraenger are only the fruit of his ingenuity which has frequent recourse to unrelated cultural spheres for explanations (e.g. he sees the snakes twisted round the harp in the Hell panel as a satire against the *fioriture* introduced into the Dutch choral singing by Josquin Desprès!), it does not seem to us that his main assumption can be dismissed. Perhaps the text of the *Miroir des simples âmes* is the closest we possess to that metaphysical Luna Park, the central panel of the *Garden of Delights*: "Why should the Soul scruple to take what she needs of the four elements, as from the brightness of the sky, the heat of fire, the freshness of water, and the earth which sustains us? Such Souls make use of all things made and created, which are needed by nature."

Perhaps Hieronymus Bosch sang in this painting his *Canticum Creaturarum*.

The Canticles of Hieronymus Bosch

Notes

[1] Beside Jurgis Baltrušaitis' *Moyen-âge fantastique, Abérrations, Anamorphoses,* we may mention Romi's *Histoire de l'Insolite,* with introduction by Philippe Soupault, Paris, Laffont, 1964; René de Solier's *L'art fantastique,* Paris, Pauvert, 1961, Roger Caillois' *Au coeur du fantastique,* Paris, Gallimard, 1965.

[2] *Nouvelle édition revue et corrigée,* 1928-1965, Gallimard.

[3] For instance Clovis Trouille, in paintings dating from 1940-1950: such as *Le Magicien, La Momie somnambule, Mon Tombeau, Justine* (reproduced by Ornella Volta, *Le Vampire,* Paris, Pauvert, 1962) adopts as a cliché a motif found in the Hell section of the *Garden of Delights,* namely the naked woman whose waist is clasped by two black hands.

[4] This motif too—a colossal, stolid face rising in an alien background—has often been used by the Surrealists, including Max Ernst and the less known Jacques Carelman in his melancholy collages of *Saroka la Géante* (Paris, Le Terrain Vague, 1965).

[5] See *The Dream* ascribed to Dosso Dossi (Dresden Art Gallery). In the same way Pushkin crowds Tatiana's dream in *Eugene Onegin* with Bosch-like monsters, c.v. stanzas 16-19.

[6] These borrowings have been illustrated by Jurgis Baltrušaitis in *Le Moyen-Age fantastique,* Paris,

Connected with the *Temptation of St. Anthony* is this sheet of pen and wash studies reproduced almost actual size [Louvre, Paris], in which the rapid stenographic notation of Bosch's late drawings assumes the character of an ideogram.

Colin, 1955, pp. 42-47, fig. 21, 22, 26. The same scholar has discussed the Oriental influences in the sixth chapter of his book. See also René de Solier, *L'Art fantastique,* p. 58.

[7] Translation by Prof. Lionel Casson, New York University.

[8] *Hieronymus Bosch,* by Charles de Tolnay, Bâle, Les Editions Holbein, 1937. New American edition, Reynal & Co., New York, 1966.

[9] *Au coeur du fantastique,* pp. 30-33.

[10] *Hieronymus Bosch, Das tausend Jährige Reich,* Grundzüge einer Auslegung, Coburg, Winkler-Verlag, 1947. The same author has given an interpretation of the *Wedding at Cana* in *Die Hochzeit zu Kana,* Berlin, 1950, which has been summarized by Enrico Castelli, *Il demonico nell'arte, Il significato filosofico del demonico nell'arte,* Milan-Florence, Electa Editrice, 1952, pp. 65-66.

[11] *Il movimento del Libero Spirito, testi e documenti a cura di Romana Guarnieri,* Rome, Edizioni di Storie e Letteratura, 1965 (fourth volume of the Archivio Italiano per la Storia della Pietà).

[12] Op. cit., p. 64.

[13] *Enciclopedia universale dell'arte,* Vol, II. column 742.

[14] *Archivio Italiano per la Storia della Pietà,* op. cit., p. 459.

[15] C. A. Wertheim-Aymès, *Hieronymus Bosch, eine Einfuhrung in sein geheime Symbolik,* Amsterdam, 1957.

[16] *Enciclopedia universale dell'arte,* Vol. II, col. 744.

V

The Moralizing Architecture of Jean-Jacques Lequeu

By André Chastel

Author

André Chastel, one of France's leading art historians, is professor of art history at the Sorbonne, head art critic of the newspaper *Le Monde,* as well as a director of the French national inventory of monuments. His books include major studies in the Renaissance and Mannerist fields. This article has been translated into English by Lane Dunlop.

Jean-Jacques Lequeu's design for a "hammock of love" in a "garden of sensual delight" is a good example of this forgotten French architect's mania for symbolically suitable structures, and of a general eighteenth-century predilection for earthly paradises.

In the degree to which man can be controlled from the outside, architecture, as a political means, deserves close study. No era had a more refined, audacious awareness of this fact than that of the French Revolution. It is primarily in the light of the "moral consequences" of architecture that one must interpret the works of those who have been called the "megalomaniacs," but who are, more exactly, the "visionaries" of architecture and not, in any case, *artistes maudits.* The key to their preoccupations is given in a projected, never-written work of Jean-Jacques Rousseau, which could have been titled "sensory morality" or "wise materialism." It is summarized in a remarkable page of the *Confessions* (II, 4), the importance of which has been pointed out by Etienne Gilson: if a man is completely dominated by his emotions and impressions, it is possible to influence his behavior only through those forms and objects which surround him and more or less obscurely touch his sensibility. Or, as so beautifully expressed by Jean-Jacques, it would be necessary "to compel our physical being to promote moral ends." Of course, he was thinking of nature and music rather than architecture. But Boullée, Ledoux and Lequeu—the last perhaps more than his colleagues—applied this idea to their own field. All the astonishing inventions of the period 1780-1800 are in fact dominated by the new ideal of "moralized architecture."

Ledoux clearly stated this in his famous *Treatise* of 1804: "If artists were willing to use the symbolic system—the form of a cube is the symbol of Justice, seated on a square stone—they would reap as much glory as poets. They would exalt the minds of all observers and not a stone in all their works would fail to speak to the eyes of the passer-by." Thus the "Pacifier," a structure designed to incite, by its very appearance, the desire for universal peace, should be a cubic block surmounted by a cylinder, on a parallelepiped base. But Ledoux is a Piranesian obsessed with formal purity. It is the abstract dignity and intractable rigor of forms that should influence the citizens' souls. Thus the absurd and ultimately immoral fantasies of "fabrications"—which Ledoux once allowed himself— are to be banished: "What contradiction! Fabrications in the Moorish or Teutonic style, or like Gothic ruins, a confusion of scenes and geography crammed within the unity of an acre of land . . ."

This indignant protest evidently refers to the projects for "symbolic" constructions which were then being produced by Lequeu. He, like Boullée, built little and imagined much. Any more than his colleagues, he did not find work with the revolutionary regimes toward which everything would have seemed to have called him. About the Year II, he drew the curious figure of a nun unveiling herself with the explicit inscription: "and you too will be mothers . . ." As has been well documented in the recent studies of G. Metke and J. Guillerme, Lequeu was extremely preoccupied with physiognomy; attentive to the possibilities of the expressive structure of facial characteristics, he tries to find complementary and opposite types. What we think of as eclecticism in his inspiration as an architect derives from the same principle. It is a question of producing models that develop, to their highest degree of effectiveness, the various "expressive" properties of architecture. Each style—Etruscan, Gothic, Chinese, Moslem—constitutes a formal system which corresponds to a "state of soul" or a dominant passion. Lequeu conducts his search to its logical end in giving unexpected, fascinating, often burlesque value to the old notion of a "speaking architecture," which has always stimulated its devotees.

Thus considered, Lequeu's bizarre enterprise seems as rich and varied as the social philosophy of a Fourier, in its ambition to establish all modes of sensibility in a monumental form, by means of associations that are sometimes startling but always definitive. Besides, like all fanatics, he turned out a profusion of legends and explanatory inscriptions intended to enlighten the novice. All the affinities of man with nature are dealt with in depth. Animal symbolism plays a large part in his grandiose Cow Barn, each of whose ornaments is drawn from bovine morphology. More puzzling is his Hen Coop, "covered with polished tin that shines in the sun," and resembling a mosque. The Exit Gate of the Hunting Grounds is appropriately surmounted with trophies which include animals: "bloodhounds, hunting greyhounds, swift and high-nosed dogs of the greatest beauty, all carved in pig-stone, a lime-like substance mixed with sulfur which, when rubbed, gives off a smell of cat's urine, rotten egg and sulfur."

Temples and fountains lend themselves endlessly to naturalistic symbolism and the exegesis of "passions." The dream of an earthly paradise, so common to the eighteenth

The Moralizing Architecture of Jean-Jacques Lequeu

A colossal statue of Amymone, one of the Danaids, dominates the "fountain of the esplanade" [left] in Lequeu's ambitious project for a "country seat."

A Gothic tabernacle [right] shelters the "frightful member" of "flirtatious Priapus," the god of gardens.

La Chasse gothique du
Dieu des jardins.

fronton à pans.

Fig. 126.

Le papillon.

flèche.

Image du
nerf érecteur.

Priape le coquet.

Membre époui

Petit de car

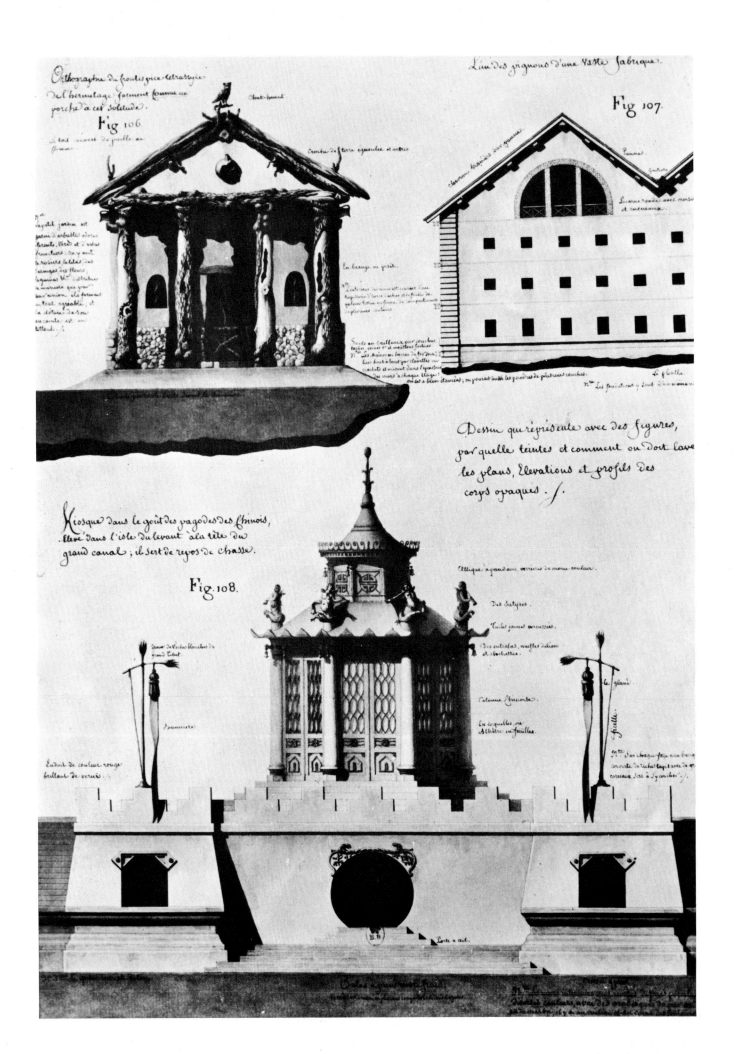

century, achieves its ultimate expression in the "abodes of pleasure": here one finds the Colossus of Amymone, one of the Danaids, inside a grotto, itself surrounded by peculiar masonry, crumpled like the folds of an accordion, while a choice place is assigned, under a Gothic tabernacle, to Priapus the Dandy, and the "hammock of love" in the little garden of voluptuousness. Complementing this is another structure: "the island of love and angler's repose, situated between the stronghold of Mars in the royal city and the fortified camp of the elite guards." The whole city is organized in this way, fulfilling all requirements: their principle is explicit, expressed in "moralized" architecture, with a view to total satisfaction.

The Temple Dedicated to the God of Armies should include, then "a divine face, disfigured by two lines, one across the forehead, the other across the nose." It is obviously derived from the esthetic of the helmet. Classic elements are omnipresent but are forced into the most extraordinary combinations by this game of psychological associations. Like all his generation, Lequeu succumbed to the fascination of the Egyptian and Etruscan; his Elevation of the Tomb of Porsenna is an impressive variant of the labyrinth theme, with "mazes built with such art that one could easily get lost." There exists in Lequeu and, as he believed, in all men and societies, an obsession with structures that dominate the individual—enveloping spaces that produce a deep unease, a sort of sacred *frisson*. This accounts for the famous projects for the Temple of Divination, the Temple of Pluto, and the underground passages for initiations. Such a repertoire inevitably included its castle of terror—an architectural counterpart of the Gothic novel and, as has been aptly noted, of *The Magic Flute* (1791): "He who will go straight ahead, without looking behind, will be purified by fire, water and air, and if he overcomes the fear of death, he will emerge from the earth, will see the light again, and will be entitled to the company of the sages, and the most courageous of men." This remarkable journey is laid

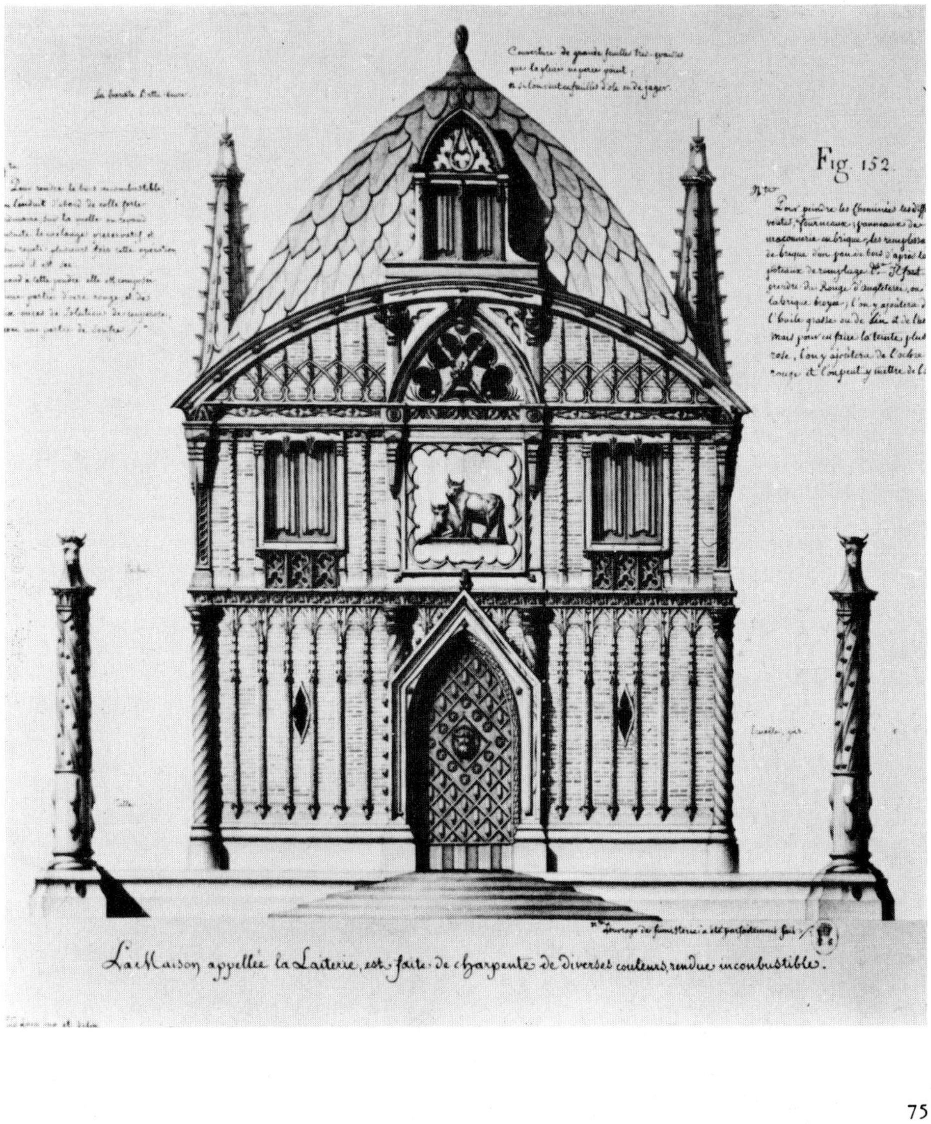

The Moralizing Architecture of Jean-Jacques Lequeu

A hermitage, a factory and a "kiosk in the style of the pagodas of the Chinese" [left] are included in this drawing, whose purpose is "to represent with figures what tints and what style should be used in wash-drawings of the planes, vertical sections and contours of opaque masses."

Dairy projected by Lequeu [right]. Ornamented with bovine sculptures, it is built of wood rendered incombustible by a formula of Lequeu's. He also suggests painting the chimneys with a mixture of crushed brick, linseed oil and urine; a pinker tint may be obtained by adding red ocher and garlic.

Fig. 152

out with meticulous attention to individual episodes. The theme of this "abode" of over-whelming surprises helps us to understand Lequeu's obsession—common to that whole epoch—with the mausoleums in which the intellectual heroes of humanity are glorified, and with graveyards conceived according to his mysterious, exact formula, as the "abode of the living."

The diversity of forms and materials projected has never, doubtless, been so suited to the vastness of the imagined themes. The singularity of these structures, the amplitude of their plans, correspond to the desire to activate to the utmost the subconscious implica-tions of architecture: Lequeu's eloquent aberrations exalt everything which the super-ficial eclecticism of the nineteenth century and the radicalism of the twentieth have constantly sought to repudiate. They stand as a kind of surrealistic protest on the threshold of industrial civilization, which has had no use for them.

Jean-Jacques Lequeu was born at Rouen, September 14, 1757. His father seems to have been a cabinet-maker or furniture designer interested in landscaping and architecture.

He attended the school of design at Rouen and was awarded prizes in 1776 and again in 1778. The director of the school, the painter Jean-Baptiste Descamps, persuaded

The Moralizing Architecture of Jean-Jacques Lequeu

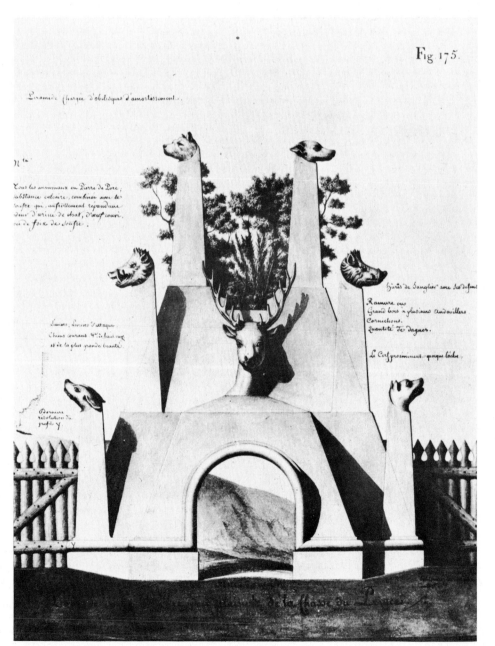

The gate of the Hunting Grounds [left] is decorated with obelisks surmounted by hunting trophies and hounds' heads "of the highest beauty."

One of Lequeu's most striking conceptions is this stable in the form of a steer [right]. The hayloft,"to be filled with hay, sainfoin and alfalfa," was to be lit by windows in the eyes of the steer.

Étable. Vache tournée au midi, est sur la fraîche prairie.

Baguette divinatoire.
Coudrier fourchu.

flamerole

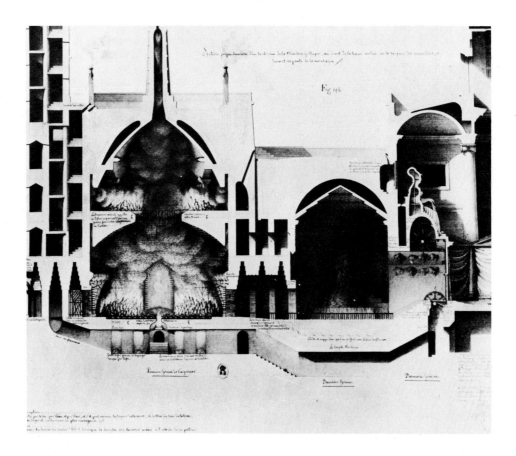

The Moralizing
Architecture of
Jean-Jacques Lequeu

Lequeu's "obsession with structures that dominate the individual" is exemplified in this project for an awe-inspiring Temple of Divination [left]. The pilasters on either side carry sculptures of forked hazel wands, symbolic of divination.

Typical of the eighteenth-century taste for the harrowing is this cross-section of Lequeu's "Maison Gothique." After trials by fire and water, as in Mozart's *Magic Flute,* the "aspirant" emerges before a colossal, machine-animated statue of Minerva [above].

The almost Surrealist architecture of the Rendezvous of Bellevue [right] is an extreme example of the "irregular houses" which were popular in France and England around 1800. A microscope and two telescopes are part of the equipment of this clifftop villa; in the sky above Lequeu has written the words *"air atmosphérique."*

Lequeu's uncle, a priest, to provide the young man with a pension for two years of study in Paris, beginning in 1779. Before leaving Lequeu designed a town hall for Rouen.

In Paris Lequeu entered the studio of the important and influential architect Jacques-Germain Soufflot, where he worked closely with Soufflot's nephew, François. Lequeu continued while in Paris to teach architectural design to students, as he had been doing at Rouen.

Sometime during the early 1780s he made the Italian tour.

In 1786, although he had continued to live in Paris, Lequeu was nominated *adjoint associé* of the *Académie Royale des Sciences, Belles Lettres et Arts* of Rouen.

Throughout the 1780s he was employed by François Soufflot as "draftsman and inspector," and also contributed designs for furniture.

With the advent of the Revolution Lequeu was forced to give up working on his own, and he became a civil servant; he had lost all his property and the times did not favor making a living by building. Lequeu entered the office of the *cadastre* (Register of Land Surveys) in 1793 and remained employed there until 1801, when the bureau was discontinued.

In 1794 Lequeu, perhaps to demonstrate his political loyalties, produced an antireligious drawing and submitted it to the Committee of Public Safety. Later he wrote on

The Moralizing Architecture of Jean-Jacques Lequeu

In 1792, at the height of the Revolution, Lequeu drew this "Elevation of the Tomb of Porsenna, King of Etruria, called the Tuscan Labyrinth" [left]. The scroll at upper left has a medallion showing a plan which is "perhaps that of the labyrinth of Crete"; at upper right is a plan of the Tuscan Labyrinth terrace.

The "Island of Love and Angler's Repose" [top right] is "located between the stronghold of Mars in the royal city and the fortified camp of the elite guard."

"Entrance to the Temple of Terpsichore, through the gallery of imitation verdure" [bottom right]. The roof of the temple is formed by a "skull-cap or parasol."

L'île d'Amour et repos de Pêche en largeur, est située entre la place de Mars de la Ville Royale, et le camp fortifié de l'élite-garde.

Entrée du Temple de Terpsichore, par
la Galerie de Verdure-feuté.

the back of it: *"Dessin pour me sauver de la Guillotine"* (Drawing to save me from the guillotine), and the ironical comment, *"tout pour la patrie."*

Lequeu secured an appointment as a cartographer in the Department of the Interior at his own request in 1801, and there he worked first on maps of Paris and later on maps of Napoleon's Empire. In 1815 he projected a Mausoleum for the Place de la Concorde, in memory of the "martyrs" beheaded there. The same year he retired with a pension.

His final years brought hardships: in 1817 he offered for sale 93 architectural drawings plus maps and his portrait, and further drawings were offered for sale in 1822 and 1824. In all cases there were no takers, despite the fact that the 1822 offer also included "eight or nine" plays he had written.

Sometime around 1825 Lequeu decided to donate all his drawings and a copy of the treatise on Chinese buildings by Chambers to the Bibliothèque Nationale. He died shortly thereafter.

His design of his tomb bears his portrait in relief, with the inscription "J. J. DEQUEUX." There is still no explanation for the misspelling. The epitaph reads:

"Sépulchre de l'auter, frère de Jésus; il a porté sa croix toute sa vie" (Sepulcher of the artist, brother of Jesus; he bore his cross throughout his life).   —Ed.

The Moralizing Architecture of Jean-Jacques Lequeu

Two curious bits of erotica by Lequeu: the nun unveiling herself [left] painted about the Year II of the Republic (1793), is labelled: "And you too shall be mothers." The lady at right wears a medallion inscribed with the word "Volupté."

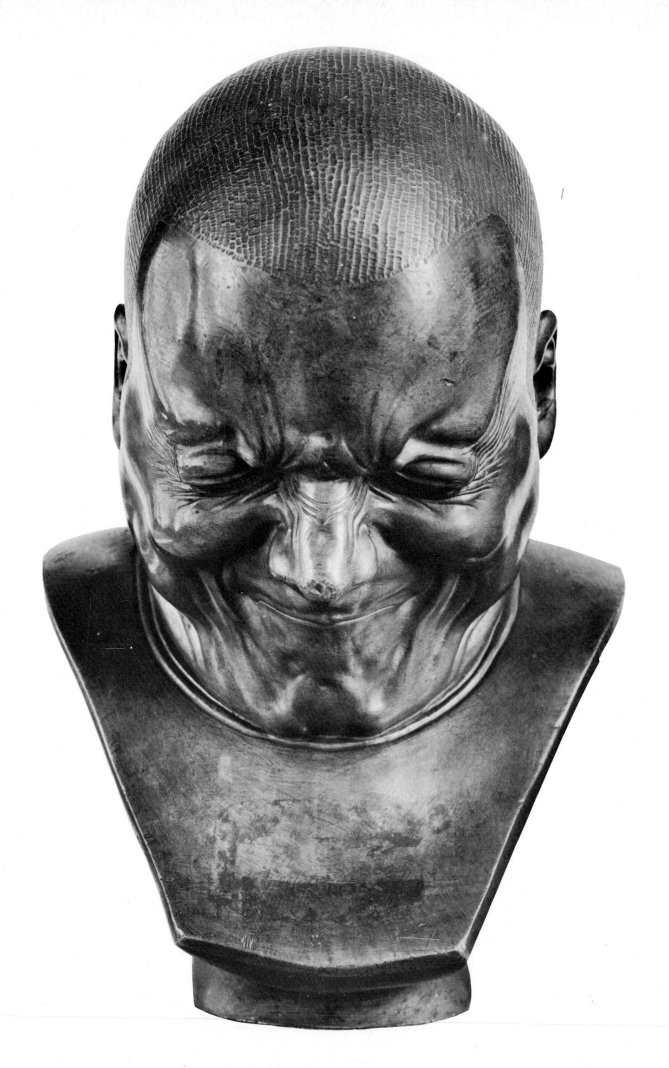

84

VI

The Artist Estranged: Messerschmidt and Romako

By Lorenz Eitner

Author

Head of the Department of Art and
Architecture and director of the museum
at Stanford University, Lorenz Eitner
is a specialist in French and
German nineteenth-century art. Of his
many publications, the most
recent is a monograph on Géricault.

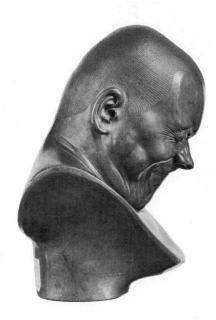

Franz Xavier Messerschmidt's *Hypocrite
Slanderer*, ca. 1780, lead, 14⅞
inches high [profile above, full-face
left]. All Messerschmidt sculptures
illustrated in this article are owned
by the Osterreichische Galerie,
in the Schloss Belvedere, Vienna.

"To be in Pressburg and not to visit the famous sculptor Messerschmidt would be a disgrace to the connoisseur of art," wrote a traveler in the early 1780s, still under the fresh impression of the "Egyptian Heads" which the unpredictable artist had allowed him to see, a privilege he did not grant to all the curious who made the tedious trip from Vienna for just this purpose. The scholar Friedrich Nicolai, luckier and more inquisitive than most, was favored by the sculptor with a detailed, if somewhat confused, explanation of these strange works and permitted to examine his small workshop on the bank of the Danube, the entire furniture of which consisted of a bed, a flute, a tobacco-pipe, a water-pitcher, an old Italian book about human proportions and the drawing of an armless Egyptian statue.

Nicolai's visit occurred in 1781. Franz Xavier Messerschmidt, once assistant professor of sculpture at the Imperial Academy of Vienna, now necromancer and recluse, was in his forty-fifth year. A robust man, of very plain appearance and manner, he had behind him a notable, though brief, career. Trained by his uncles, the brothers Johann Baptist and Philip Jacob Straub in Munich and Graz, he had continued his studies at the Vienna Academy under the celebrated Matthaeus Donner, and traveled to Rome and London in 1765. On his return, he was favored with important portrait commissions for the Imperial court and the high aristocracy of Vienna. In 1769, he was appointed to an assistant professorship at the Academy, with the expectation of promotion to the chair of sculpture at the incumbent's death. But when this occurred, in 1774, Messerschmidt was passed over, not because of intrigues against him, as he imagined, but because of a "confusion in the head" which he had suffered three years earlier and from which he still had not recovered sufficiently, according to a report to the Empress by the minister, Count Kaunitz, to qualify for the appointment. Refusing the pension which was offered him, he left Vienna, traveled in Southern Germany, vainly applied for a position at the Academy of Munich in 1775, and finally settled in Pressburg in 1777. Since the onset of his illness in 1771, he had neglected his work as a portraitist, though he still received and accepted occasional commissions, and had concentrated his great industry on the production of a series of heads of very strange aspect.

Nicolai found him busy with the sixty-first of these heads. He observed that it, like all the rest, was a self-portrait. The sculptor worked in front of a mirror. Pinching himself from time to time under the lowest right rib, he would cut a terrifying grimace, scrutinize his face in the mirror, sculpt, and after an interval of about half a minute repeat his grimace with remarkable precision. When the courteous Nicolai asked him to explain his method, Messerschmidt, somewhat hesitatingly, gave him a confused account, the gist of which can be summed up as follows: although he had lived chastely since his youth, Messerschmidt was often visited by ghosts who caused him pains in the abdomen and thighs. Fortunately, he had managed to devise a system for warding off these tormentors. This system was based on knowledge of universal proportions, learned through the study of the Egyptian Hermes Trismegistos—of whose armless statue he always kept a drawing about him. His knowledge of proportion gave Messerschmidt the power to resist the spirits. For all things have their proper proportion, and all effects come from a sufficient cause; whoever can reproduce in himself the proportions of another being should be able to produce effects equal to the effects of the other. The Egyptian Hermes is the key to the secret of proportion; it contains the norm of the human body. Head and body correspond: every part of the face, for example, is related to some other part of the body by secret analogy.

All this, in Messerschmidt's opinion, amounted to a momentous discovery which, not surprisingly, had aroused the envy of the Spirit of Proportion, the chief of his ghostly persecutors. Undaunted by the pains which the spirit inflicted on him, he resolved to delve deeper into the mystery of proportion, in order to be victorious in this contest. By observing the pains which he felt in his lower body as he worked on the faces of his busts, he came to the conclusion that if he pinched himself in different parts of the body and accompanied this with grimaces which bore the exact Egyptian proportion to the pinch, he would reach perfection in the matter of proportion. He was confirmed in his idea by an English visitor who, though unable to express himself in German, managed to convey to Messerschmidt his grasp of the principle by exposing that part of his thigh which exactly corresponded to the particular portion of the head which Messerschmidt was sculpting at the moment. Pleased with his system, Messerschmidt resolved to pass it on to posterity by means of his sculpted heads, of which he planned to execute sixty-four, since there were sixty-four canonical grimaces.

Nicolai recognized that the heads fell into three groups. There was a small number of fairly "natural" heads which showed the features of their maker slightly ennobled by a touch of stylization, or animated by fairly restrained expression, or distorted by such nor-

The Artist Estranged: Messerschmidt and Romako

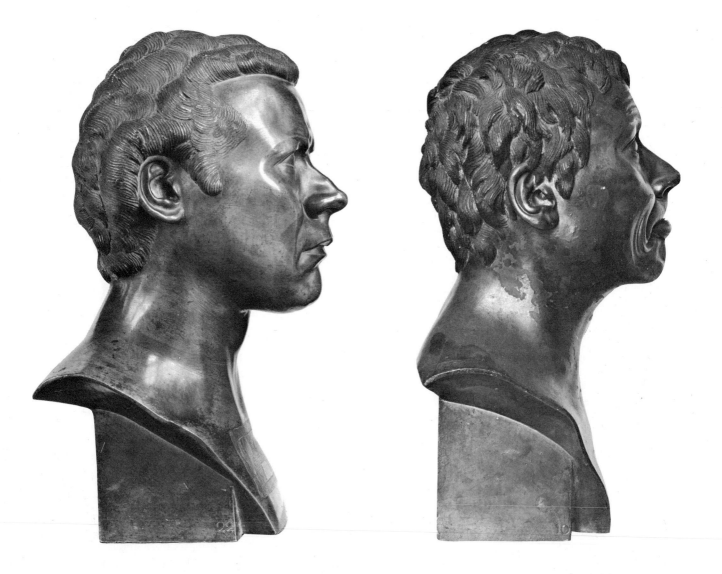

mal spasms as are produced by sneezing or yawning. In sharpest contrast to this group were two completely monstrous beak-heads in which, atop painfully extended necks, the shapes of chin, mouth and nose were thrust upward and drawn together into a sharp instrument for pecking or pinching. Messerschmidt seemed afraid of these heads and admitted to Nicolai that they represented the Spirit of Proportion. The spirit had pinched him and he had pinched back; he had finally managed to carve these two heads in marble, but had almost died in the attempt. At last, the defeated spirit had left him amidst a great stench. The third and largest group, comprising 54 busts at the time of Nicolai's visit, consisted of the convulsively grimacing heads which are still the best known of the series. All seemed to be self-portraits. Nicolai noticed that in many of them the mouths were tightly shut and the lips drawn in so as to form a thin line. Messerschmidt explained this curious feature by pointing out that men should not show the red of their lips, since animals never showed theirs—and animals, as he reminded his visitor, were superior to men in their perception of the hidden aspects of nature.

Was Messerschmidt insane? This question has aroused controversy between the psychologists and the historians. The psychoanalyst Ernst Kris who wrote two studies of Messerschmidt, the earlier of which, published in 1932, is still the most detailed account of the sculptor's work, diagnosed his case as a "psychosis with predominant paranoid trends, which fits the general picture of schizophrenia." In Kris's hands, the rather meager evidence yielded a surprisingly large and varied set of meanings. Messerschmidt's bouts with the ghosts turned out to reveal his latent homosexuality, the tightly closed lips of some of his heads to express a defensive reaction against the aggressive spirits who would force or seduce him into serving them in a female role, while the open mouths or flaccid lips of certain other heads represented a yielding to the sexual importunities of the demons. When pinching his ribs, Messerschmidt—according to Kris—acted under two

Seeking to propitiate the tormenting "Spirit of Proportion," Messerschmidt produced a series of busts ranging from the *Trustworthy Man* and *Morose Man* [left page], each lead, 17½ inches high, to such grimacing heads as *Lasciviously Languishing Fop* [below], stone, 16 inches high, climaxed by the convulsive *Beak Head*. The titles were added after the artist's death.

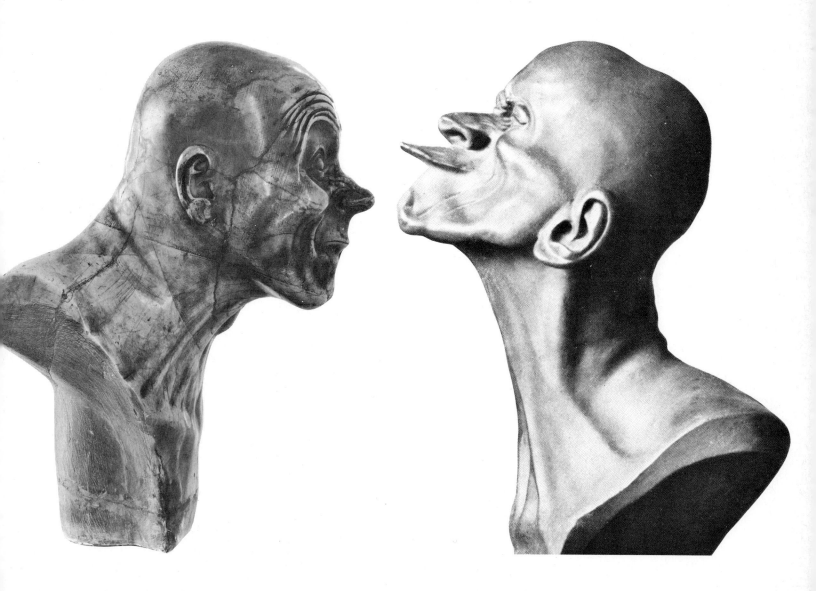

quite different impulses, "castration anxiety," on the one hand, which drove him to "prove that the rib is still there, from which God has created the woman," and, on the other hand, a megalomanic identification with God—"while working he felt his own ribs in order to create human figures."

Considered from another angle it is amusing to compare this formidable analysis with the more modest one proposed by Nicolai who, unlike the later diagnosticians, had the advantage of being personally acquainted with the patient. To this eighteenth-century materialist, the case seemed simple: Messerschmidt's sedentary life, his recurrent abdominal pains, the relief which he obtained from pinching himself under the rib cage and the bad odors which accompanied the departing tormentors proved that the sculptor's troubles stemmed from *indigestion,* complicated by his superstitious bent which made him attribute natural events to occult causes. This last defect Nicolai blamed on Messerschmidt's imagination, his solitude, gullibility and the influence of charlatans; he did not consider him to be truly mad. Modern scholars have not taken up Nicolai's suggestion, though they have leaned heavily on the rest of his account. But something akin to his humanist scepticism flavors the critique to which the art historians Rudolf and Margot Wittkower subjected Kris's psychoanalysis of Messerschmidt in their book *Born under Saturn.* They contend that, however mad Messerschmidt may have been in the opinion of modern psychiatrists, it is clear that much of his work, down to the end of his life, was entirely "normal," and that even the strange heads for which he has become famous can best be understood as works of art conditioned by an historical situation, rather than as the morbid symptoms of a solitary lunatic.

It is difficult to apply the terms of insanity or normalcy to art. Strictly speaking, their meaning is medical or social. Applied to art, they make little sense: what work of art is "normal?" What are the specific characteristics of insanity in art? Besides, like notions of beauty, notions of sanity fluctuate from one period to the next. Pressburg in 1781 tolerated Messerschmidt, just as London tolerated Blake, another seer of ghosts; today, both men would very likely be institutionalized. Certain aspects of Messerschmidt's strange personality were in his time considered to be within the bounds, or on the fringes, of convention. His belief in ghosts and methods of exorcism were no more absurd than some of the medicine or priest-craft widely practiced in his day by men reputed sane. His interest in the occult, in magic proportions and in physiognomy reflected popular pseudo-science, as propagated by such respected charlatans as Mesmer, Lavater and Gall.

But there is danger in overstressing the ties which bound him to his time. The seemingly conventional character of some of his late work is deceptive and invites misinterpretation. The magic heads, for example, are still commonly called "character heads," because they recall Lavater's physiognomic typology or because they bear a superficial resemblance to the familiar academic studies of the passions. The fanciful titles which were attached to them shortly after Messerschmidt's death represent an early attempt to minimize their uncanny strangeness. Actually, it is evident that, far from illustrating a variety of types, they repeat over and over one particular face—Messerschmidt's own. And it is equally clear that they exhibit only a very limited range of expressions, few of them corresponding to any recognizable emotion. The majority show deliberate grimaces, mask-like in their schematic artificiality. They bear out, in other words, Nicolai's account of Messerschmidt's intention, which links them more closely with primitive image magic than with eighteenth-century pseudo-science.

Messerschmidt was neither in tune with his time, nor entirely alienated from it. His artistic personality was injured, but not debilitated, by sickness; the conflict within him irritated his imagination and concentrated his energies: it was the fortunate flaw which raised his later above his earlier works and above those of his more ordinary contemporaries. Seen purely from the point of view of style and execution, the famous heads show no signs of abnormality, unless their perfect finish and Messerschmidt's deliberate choice of hard and polished materials is to be considered as perverse or obsessive. The execution is never spontaneous; even the weirdest heads are elegantly cut in marble or exquisitely cast in shining metal. Throughout the entire series, Messerschmidt's technical mastery never falters. This steadiness, this constant assurance and concentration prove that in the midst of his delusions he retained control of all his conscious resources, never falling into incoherence, rambling, or vacant embroidering. While in some details, especially of hair and skin, traces of Rococo vivacity linger, distantly recalling Messerschmidt's earlier, sumptuous court portraiture, the general treatment of the heads is bare, hard and Spartan;

The Artist Estranged: Messerschmidt and Romako

Messerschmidt's *Peevish Man,*
lead, 16¾ inches high
[above; and full-face, right].

88

seen at a distance, they remind one of the compact strength and severity of Roman portraits. They express a deliberate reaction against Baroque opulence and prove Messerschmidt to have been a pioneer of the Neo-Classical movement. Set against the background of the general history of style in their time, his bizarre heads do not appear as freaks, but as the work of a progressive and cosmopolitan artist, aware of the issues of his day. It is noteworthy that those heads of the series which are the most advanced stylistically are also the most fantastic, while the relatively "normal" ones are treated in a more conservative manner. What gives to all of them a peculiar intensity—quite apart from their obvious strangeness—is the way in which Messerschmidt has been able to combine representation with rigid stylization, expression with abstract pattern, and preserve, at the same time, both the anatomical structure and the character of portrait. To bring these divergent elements into harmony was the work of a powerful artistic intelligence.

The case of Messerschmidt proves that eccentricity, even if carried to the point of madness, can accentuate talent and promote originality so long as it does not lead to complete disorganization and breakdown. An artist trained in a great tradition and endowed with strong talent may, under the stimulus of mental disturbance, break out of school routines and current fashions to achieve something beyond his "normal" grasp. But madness or eccentricity are creative in this way only if they are brought to bear on developments or problems which exist in the realm of the normal world and affect the generality of mankind, and only if they become manifest in the work of an artist of uncommon powers, for while they can modify or stimulate, they cannot themselves produce vital art. The oddities of minor talent are sterile, though they may be of interest to the psychologist, and the spontaneous graphic expression of the untrained psychotic, *l'art brut*, the folk-art of in-

The Artist Estranged: Messerschmidt and Romako

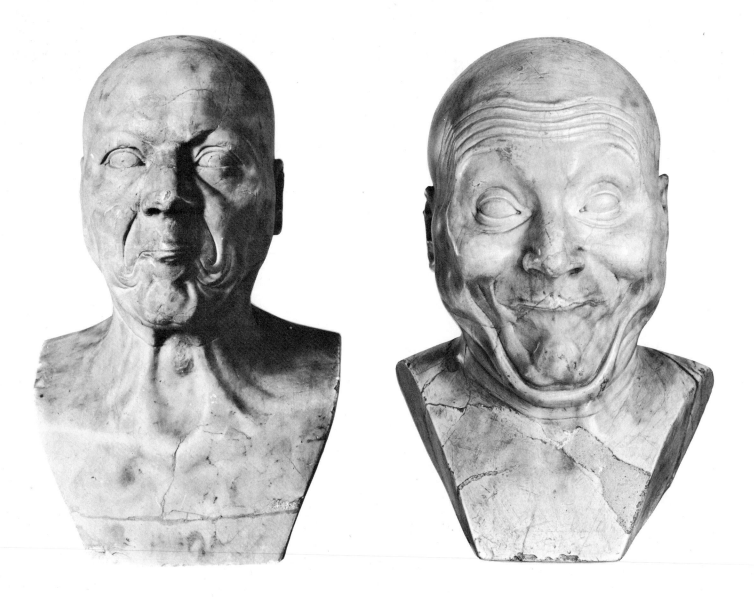

90

The only known Anton Romako in an American museum, *Girl on Swing* [above left], ca. 1882, 63 inches high, belongs to Smith College, Northampton, Mass. His *Woman in Taffeta Dress with Frills,* and all succeeding Romakos reproduced in this article are in the Osterreichische Galerie, Vienna.

Recalling Lavater's studies of physiognomy, Messerschmidt's bizarre heads were stylistically advanced for his day, anticipating Neo-Classicism in their stark forms: *Character Head* [far left], 15 inches high, and *The Consummate Rogue,* 16⅝ inches high, both marble.

sanity, exists on levels which, until the most recent present, have been isolated from the world of high art.

The career of Anton Romako (1832-1889), like that of Messerschmidt, suffered a break in mid-course: he began as a fashionable virtuoso, admired for his portraits, genres and history paintings, and ended as a haunted eccentric who was considered sick, if not insane. Having entered the Academy of Vienna at the age of fifteen, as a student of Waldmüller, whose Biedermeier naturalism did not appeal to him, he worked briefly in Munich, where he fell under the spell of Kaulbach's factitious ideality, and finished his studies in Vienna with the history painter Carl Rahl. From 1857 onward, for nearly twenty years, he settled in Rome, the favorite portraitist of foreign residents and diplomats, keeping a splendid house and acting the role of painter-prince. Much of his work throughout the 1860s consisted of anecdotal Italian genres, a highly marketable specialty, to which he applied himself with dazzling cleverness. His pictures were eagerly bought and paid well. Had he stuck to the production of picturesque *contadini* in Campagna settings, his prosperity would have remained secure, and he would be forgotten today. But there was in him a fatal restlessness, a compulsive brilliance and need to impress. He ran rapidly through a variety of styles, untroubled by technical difficulties, playing with dangerous color combinations and indulging in calligraphic extravagances. By the end of his Italian stay, he had begun to form an idiosyncratic manner which was close to the borderline of what contemporary taste would tolerate. From an agreeably conventional artist, he had evolved into an experimentalist, gradually losing touch with his public. In his landscapes, he groped toward a quasi-Impressionist luminism, while in his figure paintings he heightened expressive intensity to a point at which the character of genre or of portrait disappeared in the stress of psychological tension. *The Girl with a Basket of Fish,* painted toward the end of his Roman stay, illustrates his new, ominously expressive style which anticipated, by some ten years, Ensor's break with conventional realism.

He returned to Vienna in 1876, hoping to recapture his popularity. But he had passed

The Artist Estranged: Messerschmidt and Romako

beyond the comprehension of his contemporaries who now found his landscapes unnatural, his history paintings grotesque, his portraits ruthless. Family misfortunes aggravated his situation; his wife left him, his son suffered a mental breakdown, his two daughters, aged 16 and 19, killed themselves in 1887. Yet there is no reason to suppose that these troubles affected his artistic development, nor is there any evidence that he went out of his mind, though he was widely believed to be mad. He died a natural death in 1889, but so persistent is the conviction that unconventional work must be the product of an abnormal mind that in the literature of art his death is usually called a suicide.

Romako's late style is at its weirdest and most impressive in the portraits which he produced during the 1880s. In this branch of painting, normally the most dependent on public approval and hence the most conservative, he violated the conventions with a deliberate thoroughness which offended contemporary critics more than any headlong revolt. The supposed ugliness of his work struck them as perverse, because it was accomplished with such evident mastery and shot through with occasional disconcerting flashes of a kind of beauty which they could recognize. They found in Romako's portraits something of caricature mixed with flattery, a strident exaggeration of current fashions and affectations, a note of *kitsch*. Worst of all, to the anxious middle-class mind, his paintings seemed in dubious taste. The only public left to him in the end were a few emancipated souls and a handful of aristocrats indifferent to notions of taste.

The *Portrait of Isabella Reisser,* 1885, can still shock, though its eccentricities have lost their novelty. In its time, it was a scandal. The marionette-like stiffness of the figure, the decorative angularities of its silhouette, the face in straight front view, the most unflattering imaginable, and the archaic hardness of the features: were they to be taken as the expression of naïveté or of decadence? Was the drawing of the face really as bad as it seemed, or in its way perversely clever? In *The Two Friends,* ca. 1880, these annoying ambiguities went even further. Romako seemed to have omitted nothing that might startle or offend. Bright, intense, strident colors, instead of the familiar brown juice; surfaces teeming with detail, without any suggestion of atmosphere or space; and, throughout, a vivid unwholesomeness—it was difficult to tell whether the image was intended to suggest reality or fantasy, whether it was to be taken literally or as satire. With equal ease, one might read into these paintings the indictment of a society, or find in them merely the morbid vision of Romako, whom one critic had called "the sick man of art."

To the very end, he retained the versatility which had marked his early work. He tried repeatedly to apply his radical new style to the most obsolete of subject matters—history painting—that sacred bore which had been the undoing of many artists in the nineteenth century. For his most ambitious effort in this vein, he chose a modern episode, *Admiral Tegetthoff at the Battle of Lissa,* an incident of the Austro-Italian war of 1866, which he painted in three different versions about 1880. His intention was to give monumental form to an event taken from contemporary life, very much as Manet had done in his *Execution of Maximilian.* But while Manet sought inspiration in Goya, Romako experimented with a completely original compositional device, spacing his figures in two superimposed zones and silhouetting them against the flat, light ground. The strangeness of this arrangement, and the odd, unheroic stance of the Admiral provoked a savage reaction from the critics.

As Fritz Novotny has shown, in *Der Maler Anton Romako* (1954), Romako's work was not without parallels in its time. In the broadest sense, it belonged to a general reaction against naturalism, the effects of which were felt throughout Europe and particularly in France. The crisis in Romako's development during the 1870s corresponded to the widespread search for a new style which was to be more expressive and more abstractly decorative than the various forms of realism then current. It is possible to classify his work as being on the periphery of Post-Impressionism. Despite its very marked individuality, it contains some surprising analogies to other work of the time, to certain portraits by van Gogh, for instance, which show heads in front view against violently patterned backgrounds. Romako has been called a precursor of Expressionism; his mannerist calligraphy and his peculiar colorism connect him more closely with Art Nouveau and, beyond it, with the styles of Klimt, Schiele and Kokoschka.

Even to modern eyes, Romako's late paintings often seem shrill. His stylizations have a vehemence, an edge of aggressiveness, which the literal content of the pictures does not explain. They reflect the bitterness of artistic controversies, the points of which have long since been forgotten, and perhaps a larger hostility toward a world in which he no longer

A scandal in its day:
Portrait of Isabella Reisser, 1885, by Anton Romako, called by one critic, "the sick man of art."

felt at ease. Much in his style appears to stem from systematic contradiction. Where accepted painting usage called for elegant fudging, as in the backgrounds of portraits, Romako painted teeming detail, microscopically distinct and hard as flint. Where common usage called for atmosphere and space, he built walls of agitated ornament. He caused the distances to come forward, and near forms to recede; he smothered his figures in their surroundings, or set them starkly against a blank.

The vehemence with which Romako repudiated artistic conventions was probably sharpened by his knowledge that this repudiation included his own earlier work, and amounted to a sacrifice of success, position, even livelihood. Romako's fall was not the unavoidable consequence of his development of a personal style, it was the result of his turning against the taste of the society which had patronized him. In forming the eccentric style of his late years, he exiled himself from the world of approval and success, not unlike Messerschmidt, a century earlier. In the opinion of contemporaries, such a withdrawal indicated abnormality. The irony of history has reversed this estimate. In the modern view, the original artist, working for himself, and drawing his ideas from private fantasy appears as the more significant and, in this sense, more "normal" figure than the successful society painter or the sculptor of the Imperial Academy. The eccentrics of the past anticipated the present norm.

The Artist Estranged:
Messerschmidt and Romako

In genre like *The Two Friends* [right], ca.1880, the ambiguities of Romako's late style seemed like deliberate indictments of contemporary society.

In Romako's early fashionable Academic manner: *Girl with Soap Bubbles.*

VII

Sir John Soane: Museum or Mausoleum?

By John Jacobus

Author

John Jacobus has completed a book on the architecture of Philip Johnson; his volume on Victorian building is in press, and he is currently finishing a book on Matisse. He teaches history of art at the University of Indiana.

A bust of Sir John Soane (by his friend Sir Francis Chantrey) gazes out over part of his collection of antique fragments in "The Dome," the focal point of the bizarre residence Soane designed for himself in Lincoln's Inn Fields, London. Funerary urns and sarcophagi set the somewhat lugubrious tone of this room, the earliest to be constructed (1808-09).

"I had again and again contemplated that person's dwelling place, a very odd shell, denoting the abode of a very 'odd fish.' " The dwelling place in question was outwardly a Georgian brick and stone façade on the north side of Lincoln's Inn Fields, London. Its occupant and creator was the architect Sir John Soane, R. A., born London 1753, died there 1837. Like most prominent English architects from the time of Inigo Jones, Soane was a striking individualist, the heir of an insular tradition in architectural invention that had produced a series of brilliant if often unclassifiable mavericks: Wren, John Vanbrugh, Nicholas Hawksmore and Robert Adam, not to mention two of Soane's contemporaries, James Wyatt, creator of William Beckford's neo-Gothic fantasy at Fonthill, and John Nash, the builder of Oriental fantasies at Brighton as well as only slightly more sober-minded Neo-Classic terrace houses about the edges of London's scenic parks.

Soane's architecture, of which his own house in Lincoln's Inn Fields is one of the few unspoilt, relatively intact specimens to survive into our own day, virtually defies description or even concise verbal characterization. Almost in despair, Prof. Hitchcock has employed the awkward, if certainly onomatopoetic adjective "Soanic," which, after a certain acquaintance with the man's work, serves not only as a description of Soane's own style, but, equally, of a certain stubborn linear harshness that has sporadically cropped up in much subsequent English building from the Victorian era through that of the Arts and Crafts and Art Nouveau, and is today very much present in the strikingly different British architecture of the third quarter of the twentieth century.

More helpful to the neophyte, however, is the crustaceous metaphor of George Wrightwick's description, "a very odd shell," a somewhat deprecatory way of characterizing the sensitive, emotional man who successfully cloaked himself with his buildings, becoming, in his last years (like, in our own day, Wright and Le Corbusier), an old man mad about architecture, and around whose person the vision and reality of that art is ultimately drawn like a shroud. In the words of Sir John Summerson, "He was not, in the ordinary sense, a happy man, nor would he for one moment have desired posterity to think that he was. But he loved architecture as few Englishmen have loved it and, in this intense absorption, earned the indescribable felicity of the discoverer."

Although Soane was an architect of that late Georgian epoch whose ultimate blandishments of taste and eccentricity have gone down in history as "Regency Style," he was neither its creature nor its creator, but rather a lone outsider. To the traveled or bookish eye, his house and its contents, conceived during his lifetime to become a museum after his death, "dates" with perfect ease into its period, the second decade of the nineteenth century. There is nothing about Soane's "Museum-House" to make it fundamentally a precursor of our contemporary technologically oriented styles, as was to be the case with so many of the glass and iron conservatories and train sheds built within a generation of its completion. Its particular timelessness does not depend upon the timeliness of its arrival on the architectural scene. Rather, its uniqueness is due to the architect's omniscience weaving together several historical threads into a totally distinctive fabric. At a time when the mnemonic revivals of Greek and Gothic were in full bloom, Soane did not turn his back, but rather his mind engulfed this material and, thanks to his solitary vision, made something new of it. In the seventh lecture of a series delivered before the Royal Academy he stated: "Architecture is an art purely of Invention (as opposed to Imitation in painting and sculpture), and Invention is the most painful and most difficult exercise of the human mind."

Needless to say, the remark must be read in the spirit of the time. By referring parenthetically to "Imitation" as a method not fit for architects, he seems to be respectfully chiding those among his contemporaries whose most seductive building designs were produced by imitative efforts parallel to those of a Neo-Classic sculptor like Flaxman or a Neo-Classic painter like Benjamin West. Such facile practices never crept into Soane's work, even during his early maturity, and we may indeed believe that it was poignantly, personally true that for him invention was "the most painful and the most difficult exercise of the human mind." Unlike certain artists, who go to great pains to conceal the difficult steps in the evolution of a given form, thereby giving the illusion of spontaneity, Soane's architecture, even his simplest, most barren constructions, are pock-marked with their creator's trials and frustrations.

Soane's preferences for certain architects in the British tradition, notably his admiration for the architect of Blenheim Palace, Sir John Vanbrugh (whose buildings if not whose plays he considered on a par with Shakespeare), provide a clue to the way in which he reinterpreted the styles of the past in his own house. These passions indicate the font from which he evolved his austere, astringent taste, one which was acid enough to level out and equalize some of the most differentiated building styles in all history. "For invention [Vanbrugh] has no equal in this country," observed Soane. "Boldness of Fancy, unlimited Variety and Discrimination of Character mark all his productions . . . The young Architect, by studying the picturesque effects of his works will learn to avoid the dull monotony of minor artists, and be led to think for himself and acquire a taste of his own."

Soane's own house is, in its final form, primarily a museum. As an office and habitation during the architect's later years, particularly after his wife's death in 1815, the building could scarcely be described as functional in the ordinary domestic sense, in spite of the presence of innumerable structural and decorative innovations of a most ingenious sort. Not only does a museum-leitmotif dominate Soane's last residence; it manages this with a certain funerary aura to which both the architecture itself and the remarkable collection, with its splendid Egyptian sarcophagus of Seti I, centrally installed in a "Sepulchral Chamber" (the architect's designation), make complementary, interlocking contributions.

Soane's "dwelling" at 13 Lincoln's Inn Fields of 1812-13 was, in fact, the second residence constructed by the architect for himself on that square. The first, next door at number 12, was built in 1792, after he had been practicing professionally in London for a decade, and four years after he had been appointed to his most challenging and prestige-laden position as architect to the Bank of England. Not quite a decade later he acquired a country seat: Pitzhanger Manor on Ealing Green (presently a borough public library), which he purchased in 1800. Designed in 1770 by George Dance the Younger, Soane's sometime employer at that epoch, Pitzhanger possibly possessed a certain nostalgic significance for the successful middle-aged architect when he moved in at the turn of the century. Moreover, the architecture of George Dance, with its ingenious, personal variants created within the classical repertoire of domes, pendentives and columns, was perhaps the most crucial formative influence upon Soane, providing him with both structural and spatial themes for his own even more imaginative vaulted interiors.

Pitzhanger was gradually rebuilt both inside and out during Soane's ownership, which ended in 1811, although one of Dance's interiors was carefully preserved. The back parlor and front parlor are remarkable for their handsome ceilings representing, respectively, a groin vault and a dome. Both ceilings have a drastically flattened curvature, so that a shell-like surface effect results. Outside, in addition to a columned triumphal-arch façade in the tradition of Robert Adam's at Kedleston, but with certain eccentric variations, Soane created a sham ruin which testifies to his devotion to the morbid eighteenth-century fascination with decay and desolation. Pitzhanger was in many ways a first study of certain spatial and expressive ideas that would ultimately be incorporated in the second, definitive Lincoln's Inn Fields house of 1812-13, even though the primary function of his country retreat was as a setting for the brilliant social and artistic assemblies in which

Sir John Soane: Museum or Mausoleum?

The façade of Sir John Soane's Museum, 13 Lincoln's Inn Fields [top left]. Despite its conservative look, incorporated fragments of Gothic stonework and Greek statuary hint at the eccentricity of the interior.

A fragment of the "canopy" in the Dining Room [top right]. Mirrors are used to give the illusion that the ceiling is repeated in another room. On the bottom right pedestal is a bust of the poet and essayist William Dodd, executed in 1777 for forgery.

"Monumental architecture on a doll's house scale": the Study and the tiny Dressing Room, with windows overlooking the Monument Court and the Monk's Yard [bottom right].

The Breakfast Room [bottom left]. Of this room and the complex vistas opening from it, Soane wrote that he had tried to "present a succession of those fanciful effects which constitute the poetry of architecture."

Sir John Soane:
Museum or Mausoleum?

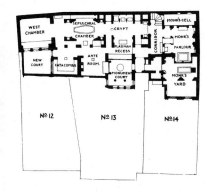

Plan of the Basement.

The Monk's Yard, whose "ruins" are a hodgepodge of fragments from buildings which Soane was instrumental in demolishing. At center is the tomb of "Padre Giovanni," Soane's *alter ego*.

Soane and his wife indulged at the time, whereas the later house was the lair of a solitary, misanthropic genius, destined ultimately to become a museum as well as his spiritual mausoleum.

If Pitzhanger was mainly triumphal and festive, 13 Lincoln's Inn Fields was introverted, melancholic and other-worldly—as well as autobiographic. Soane obtained the freehold in 1811, and in 1812-13 he completely reconstructed the premises, detaching certain rooms from the rear of his earlier residence at number 12 (such as the "Dome" of 1809, first constructed as an annex of number 12, although in fact situated in the garden of number 13 which he had leased for the purpose) and incorporating them in the new house. Hence it is all but impossible to make sense of number 13 as a conventional entity, since the plan is a collage-like agglomeration of various rooms designed or remodeled at different periods as parts of different ensembles, with the result that the house as it stands is no more unified in the classical sense than is the plot of a Gothic novel. Soane himself, in his privately-printed *Description of the House and Museum on the North Side of Lincoln's Inn Fields*, first published in 1830, apologizes, noting that the various parts were purchased at various times. Therefore he was, in his own words, "unable . . . to construct the whole on a general plan, forming one unified pile, well balanced in all its parts." And as if to make even more explicit his embarrassment and self-criticism he cites the admonition of the eighteenth-century French commentator, Abbé Marc-Antoine Laugier, whose rational architectural doctrine played a considerable role in the evolution of Soane's idiosyncratically simple, linear derivations from the classical repertoire: " 'If there is something which is due to the invention of the architect, it is the plan of the edifice. It is there that he has the opportunity of displaying his creative gifts, through combinations that are always different and always equally correct.' " Yet the irregular, partly fortuitous layout of Soane's house, like those of his now-mutilated, large-scaled masterpiece, the Bank of England, or his destroyed halls and chambers at Westminster, is basic to its virtue and appeal. Part of his strength and distinctiveness as a designer resides in the fact that his spaces had to be tailored to accord with some pre-existent structure, and these spaces were furthermore usually designed and built piecemeal. Soane's genius results from the dilemma that he encountered between the demands of Neo-Classic idealism on the one hand, and the peculiar material demands that his sites and situations forced upon him on the other.

However, the plan of Soane's house is not what strikes the spectator first, and, indeed, once inside the eye is so busy taking in so many other novel features that it is some time before one comes to wonder about the rationale of the layout at all, except as it concerns the invariably ingenious relationship between any one particular room and its immediate neighbor. The exterior façade *seems* straightforward enough, distinctive but not peculiar to the unpracticed twentieth-century eye. (The adjacent house-fronts at numbers 12 and 14, are, in fact, subsidiary flanking parts integral with the central composition of 13, even though they contain separate dwellings.) "The front of the house is of Portland stone and brick," is the laconic way in which Sir John Summerson opens his *New Description of Sir John Soane's Museum* (1955), features that are scarcely remarkable given the date and place. Only gradually does the exceptional monumentality of the centermost of the three unified façades make itself felt to contemporary sensibilities, so subtly detailed and cleverly proportioned are the Portland stone projections (originally the *piano nobile* boasted an open loggia—providing the façade with greater distinctiveness, perhaps—but this space was made into a glass-enclosed part of the drawing room behind in 1834, three years before the architect's death). The weirdness of this planar composition registers only when the visitor strolls around to the adjacent side of Lincoln's Inn Fields to discover two well-turned house designs, one of the seventeenth and one of the eighteenth century, in the correct, orthodox academic formula of Inigo Jones. With this effective reminder of classicizing norms, one returns to puzzle out Soane's stark, round-arched forms and incised decorative motifs. At last the point becomes clear: the unusual proportions and abrupt changes of scale were not the result of peevishness nor of gratuitous seeking after novelty. Two figures in cast stone, derived from the porch of the maidens at the Erechtheum, are placed atop the stone cornice of the *piano nobile,* while beneath, large as life (and just as real) four Gothic corbel blocks, shaped like foliate capitals, which originally formed a part of the fourteenth-century façade of Westminster Hall, are set into the walls between the windows. They obey no structural logic as they would have in their original situation, nor does their placement conform to classical canons of design, although they do punctuate the flat-surfaced façade in an important if unusual way. Their function is explanatory rather than structural or even decorative: The beholder is formally warned not to expect classical or even rational consistency either here on the exterior or in the interior. Indeed, we may fairly assume that the distinctive proportions of the façade are in part contrived in a Gothic spirit, even when the form is altogether something else . . . In his tenth lecture to the Royal Academy Soane asks, "Why should we not unite the variety of Figure, the wild effects, the bold combinations of cultivated Art, with all the regularity displayed in Ancient Architecture?" Following in the footsteps of certain pioneering eighteenth-century designers, he was eager to welcome the improvised freshness and emotional suggestiveness of Gothic buildings into contemporary design, without, however, borrowing the exact letter of its forms, except for certain limited, specific purposes—as will be seen in the Monk's Yard, one of the two interior courtyards of 13 Lincoln's Inn Fields.

Entering, the visitor passes swiftly through hall and staircase to the Dining Room, which with the Library "may be considered as one room, being separated only by two projecting piers formed into bookcases, from which springs a canopy of three segmental arches" (Soane). This suite of rooms, constructed in 1812-13, is well lit from windows in the library facing to the front and from windows in the Dining Room facing the "Monument Court," a central open space scarcely larger than a light well, but crammed full of all sorts of architectural memorabilia. "From this window," continues the architect, "The Monument Court, with its architectural pasticcio, and assemblage of ancient and modern art . . . are seen to great advantage." Some of the fragments from this collection have been removed, including the tower-like pasticcio itself, but numerous bits and pieces from various old buildings demolished during Soane's lifetime still are to be seen. The collection in this courtyard, together with the heterogeneous grouping of art objects in the Library and Dining Room, effectively points up the fragmentary nature of the spaces in the house, many of which are tiny, and the mixed nature of the decorative motifs employed. In these two relatively large ground-floor rooms, for example, the over-all classical tone of a typical Regency interior is spiced with columnar details that are suggestively Egyptian and Gothic, while the segmental arches separating the two rooms are a kind of meringue meant to suggest the profiles of Gothic pendant vaults, without however serving any structural function.

Extending to the rear of the house, flanking the sides of the Monument Court, are, at the left, a medium-sized, rectangular Breakfast-Parlor and, at the right, a miniature suite of two square spaces scarcely wider than a ship's companionway, the Study and the Dressing Room, both with walls and ceilings of considerable architectonic interest given their diminutive size. The Dressing Room possesses a window that looks out on one side towards the Monument Court and a second which overlooks the Monk's Yard, a touchingly Romantic, largely Gothic pasticcio, whose significance is tied to the Monk's Parlor and Cell in the basement (q.v.). Opposite the Monument Court, and opening from the left rear of the Dining Room, is the Breakfast Parlor, the most monumental and recognizably Classic of the interiors designed by Soane for his ultimate residence. It is roofed with a flattened dome that forms a continuous, concave, shell-like surface with its four pendentives—"a spherical ceiling, springing from four segmental arches, supported by the same number of pilasters, forming a rich canopy," says Soane. And, in case the visitor has not observed the multitude of vistas that open beyond (and above), he continues: "The views from this room into the Monument Court and into the Museum [more specifically, the Dome], the mirrors in the ceiling, and the looking glasses, combined with the variety of outline and general arrangement in the design and decoration of this limited space, present a succession of those fanciful effects which constitute the poetry of architecture." In addition to the light received into the Breakfast Parlor from ordinary window sources, there is an oculus with a lantern-light in the center of the dome or "spherical ceiling," and, at the far end of the room, nearest the Museum, there is a concealed source of light high above the concave surface of the ceiling, which produces a strong highlight against the rear wall, through which glazed doors open onto the Museum proper, where we perceive a completely distinct sky-lit space.

Fascination with light and shadow, borrowed from his knowledge of antique and Roman baroque precedents, and equally traceable to his acquaintance with Piranesi, accounts for only a part of these tantalizing, miniaturized architectural effects. Indeed, Soane's cleverness almost gets out of hand. Yet where a lesser talent would have produced

Sir John Soane: Museum or Mausoleum?

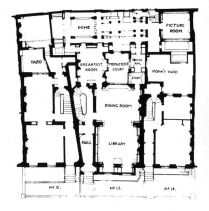

Plan of the ground floor.

The South Drawing Room, on the first floor [top]: door at right leads to a loggia running the length of the façade. Originally open, it was later enclosed by Soane. The portrait of Soane is by William Owen; the bust on the bookcase at right is of Palladio.

Kept almost exactly as it was in Soane's lifetime, the Dining Room [bottom] shows his predilection for mingling Classical and Gothic motifs. Lawrence's portrait of Soane hangs over the fireplace, and on the mantelpiece is a model for the architect's largely unrealized project for the Board of Trade and Privy Council Offices, Whitehall.

Sir John Soane:
Museum or Mausoleum?

The Picture Room [top left] is notable
both for its fine collection of paintings
(including Hogarth's *Rake's Progress*
series) and for its architectural
innovations. The hinged panels were
invented to house Soane's large collection;
they open to reveal a light well
overlooking the Monk's Parlor.

The Crypt, looking west [top right]. At
right is a cast of the Medici Venus; in
the background is the Sepulchral Chamber
with the sarcophagus of King Seti I,
discovered in 1815 at Thebes. Soane
acquired it in 1824, and held a
three-day reception in its honor.

The Colonnade, looking east [bottom
left]. The cupboards at left and right
originally contained Soane's collection
of 53 volumes of drawings by the
architects Robert and James Adam.

The Corridor [bottom right], adjacent to
the Monk's Parlor, in the basement.
Among the antique marbles and casts is
a fragment of a child's sarcophagus.

redundant clutter, he manages the near-impossible, perhaps because he had already conceived and built many of these shapes at a more normal, monumental scale in his large projects, like the Bank of England, before he came to the design of his own house. In this way, his house becomes a kind of retrospective architectural model, grouping together in a small space effects that normally would be employed in public buildings of considerable size. In Soane's residence we are experiencing monumental architecture at doll's-house scale, as, with a strange premonition, the architect gives us a world in a looking glass—"A very odd shell" indeed. Much as a Roman Emperor, Hadrian, had in his villa at Tivoli grouped together architectural effects that he had discovered in his travels over much of the ancient world, Soane brought together in his own house motifs gathered from many of the same sources, but here filtered through the deep recesses of a mind obsessed with Invention.

The principal axis of the Museum spaces runs at right angles to that of the rooms already described (although several minor cross-axes of the Museum are tied to the principal axis and its parallels from the front, thereby weaving the whole together in a picturesque rather than in an academic, a Vanbrugian rather than a Palladian manner). These Museum spaces occupy the garden areas of numbers 12 and 14 as well as 13, although, in the final ordering of things, the fronts of these two plots contained separate houses. Furthermore, these exhibition spaces were either constructed before the principal building campaign of 1812-13 which resulted in the already-discussed rooms of number 13 (and were thus conceived as extensions to his earlier residence of 1792 at number 12) or were constructed afterwards, in large measure to accommodate the growing collection housed in this eccentric residence, which despite its heterogeneous style, ultimately became an almost Pharaonic series of tomb-chambers where a multitude of art objects were being piled up to serve the needs of his architecture in a life beyond the tomb—indeed to provide the very excuse by which Soane could insure the survival of his alchemic architectural invention.

The architectural history of the museum leads from west to east, or, facing the rear of the property, from left to right. As the concept took root in Soane's mind, and since the space at his disposal was severely limited, the basement area was incorporated with the ground floor (which, at one point, includes a kind of mezzanine), the spaces bound together vertically by shafts and light-wells designed with the same compositional ingenuity as that with which the various elements of the plan were woven together in the front of the house. What Soane did earlier in two dimensions, he achieved in three dimensions in the Museum proper, creating to the scale and volume of chamber music a dense, suffocating agglomeration of spaces that parallels the effects of scale versus monumentality in the late quartets and sonatas of Beethoven. The saving grace—the safety valve—of Soane's Museum is the series of glass domes and vaults: a complex of skylights which vertically extend the space, giving it the airiness of Gothic proportions while preserving, however attenuated, its classical syntax.

The Dome is the focal point of the Museum as finally constituted, as well as its oldest portion, having been constructed, as we have seen, in 1808-09 as a Model Room (part of his professional office) attached to the rear of number 12, though in fact situated in the garden (which he had leased) of number 13. Strictly speaking, this Dome is nothing more than an iron and glass conical skylight surmounting a space with an open, balustraded floor looking directly into the basement. However, this centralizing volume is sufficiently suggestive to justify the term, albeit as something of a conceit. By 1813, as testified by a drawing of his pupil James Gandy, the Dome with its integral basement, ultimately destined to become the Sepulchral Chamber in 1824, was crammed with an extraordinary collection of antiquities, some, of course, no more than casts, and others heavily restored. Not the least curious fact about this collection was that various items were formerly in the hands of other architects: Lord Burlington, Robert Adam and even Piranesi. Funerary urns and fragments of sarcophagi already attest to the morbid nature of the place, an other-worldly orientation which will ultimately crystallize about the Belzonni Sarcophagus of Seti I. This treasure was acquired in 1824 and installed in the lower, basement portion of the Dome, thenceforth known as the Sepulchral Chamber— evoking with its aura of Nilotic mystery the ideals of Freemasonry, much as Mozart had done earlier in his *Magic Flute*.

On the ground floor, a Colonnade connects the Dome with the Picture Room, built in 1824 in the yard behind the separate house at number 14, which Soane also rebuilt in this year, having apparently obtained that property in 1811. Above this Colonnade, which is barely 8 feet high, a working space for draftsmen, known as the Student's Room, was constructed, and indeed this light structure is all that is borne by these somewhat massive, bizarrely proportioned Corinthian columns, whose bulk is almost Romanesque in flavor. In the Basement the Sepulchral Chamber underneath the Dome opens into the Crypt (below the Colonnade), and leads to the Monk's Parlor below the Picture Room, which the architect referred to as the "Parloir [sic] of Padre Giovanni." This monastic chamber faces out into the Monk's Yard, with its ruined cloister (whose stones came from the window embrasures of the House of Lords, Westminster, torn down in 1823 to make way for a new Royal Gallery designed by Soane himself) and the Monk's Tomb (which is a hodgepodge of various fragments).

Its creator, whom we should not shrink from identifying as Padre Giovanni himself, describes this flotsam and jetsam: "The ruins of a monastery arrest the attention. The interest created in the mind of the spectator, on visiting the abode of the monk, will not be weakened by wandering among the ruins of his once noble monastery . . . which cannot fail to produce the most powerful sensations in the minds of the admirers of the piety of our forefathers, who raised such structures for the worship of the Almighty Disposer of events." The frailty of human existence is here represented through the fragile remains of other buildings from other times—fragments turned up not at random, but from buildings that Soane himself was in some way instrumental in destroying, since it was he who was creating their successors. One senses in the ultimate meaning of the Monk's Parlor and Yard a premonition of the cruel fates that would oversee the destruction or mutilation of the major part of his own life's work within a century of his death. In that respect, the Museum he built as his own last earthly residence is the explicit realization of the sentiments so touchingly expressed in the Monk's Yard, since it was, among other things, the repository of his own drawings of his buildings and projects. A tortuous complex of motives, a determination that his voice and message should be heard beyond the tomb, beyond even the mortal lifespan of his monumental constructions at the Bank of England and at Westminster, explains the nature as well as the very existence of his house.

Above the Monk's Parlor is the climactic room of the museum, both from the point of view of architecture and from that of the collection itself: the Picture Room, constructed simultaneously with the apartment of Padre Giovanni, and which actually forms a part of the same spatial ensemble when the hinged wall panels of the Picture Room are opened, since behind these panels is a shallow recess, about 5 feet across, extending the full width and height of the room, which opens directly into the front part of the Monk's Parlor immediately below. In a most recondite fashion, the architect has employed a two-story light-well to expressively link together two spaces, one above the other. The ceiling of the Picture Room is a phantasmagorical combination of classic and Gothic motifs blended in a series of arched pendant canopies. Soane's levitational exercise here—a process in which normally load-bearing classical forms are made to perform acrobatic feats analogous to late medieval pendant vaults—is the ultimate development of his tendency to conceal the compressive nature of load-bearing structures. The dome of his Breakfast Parlor, itself taken over from the Front Parlor of his earlier country residence at Pitzhanger Manor, was a drastically flattened saucer shape, whose curve was so shallow that Soane preferred to call it a spherical ceiling, and with good reason. Forms as well as objects in Soane's house are not simply what they seem to be at first glance, but are, in addition, allusions to their owner and to his fascination with strange and suggestive transformations.

As for the remarkable picture collection, it includes Hogarth's eight paintings of *The Rake's Progress,* acquired in 1802 for Pitzhanger, where they must have provided a slight if characteristically caustic comment on the brilliant round of entertainments that Soane undertook at that epoch. As for the four pictures of *The Election,* Soane bought these Hogarth masterpieces from Mrs. Garrick, whose husband had acquired them directly from the artist, for the considerable sum of 1650 guineas in 1823. These narrative and moralistic scenes are surrounded by countless architectural views and fantasies by Piranesi, Clérisseau and Pannini. When these outside, or front, wall panels are opened up they reveal, heretofore completely hidden, what would normally be the contents of another room and more (the artifice of this concealment is one of the ultimate delights of Soane's necropolean dwelling). On these inside panels are innumerable architectural renderings of

Soane's own buildings, some from the hand of his pupil, James Gandy, among which is an extensive fantasy titled "Architectural Visions of Early Fancy . . . and Dreams in the Evening of Life" (ca. 1820), a watercolor that brings together the design that earned him the Royal Academy Gold Medal in 1776 as well as certain later designs which, as he could never execute them, were among his deepest regrets. Touchingly, these and other projects lie buried behind the moralistic paintings of Hogarth and the architectural schemes of others.

The upper floors are not of the same interest. The first floor (i.e. the one above the ground floor, or, from the exterior, the *piano nobile*) contains but two amply proportioned drawing rooms placed over the Library and the Dining Room. The second, or "Chamber," floor was given over to three bedrooms, but these have been somewhat altered, now serving as offices and study rooms. If these were the architect's actual lodgings (he died in the back bedroom on January 20, 1837), his spiritual abode is down below: in the Parlor of Padre Giovanni, in the Dome and Picture Room, in the Breakfast Parlor and in the Library; in every brick and treasure that was lovingly accumulated over a forty-five year period beginning with his first acquisition of property at number 12 in 1792.

George Wrightwick, who had briefly served as scribe to Soane in 1826-27, and who had likened the house to the shell of a very odd fish, seems to have put his finger upon the cranky peevishness, indeed pathetically misanthropic nature of Soane's style, mirroring but not mimicking his personality, as it gradually evolved away from even the boldest variations of his masters like Henry Holland and George Dance the Younger, or his contemporaries like James Wyatt and John Nash: "So far as his structures proclaim him," wrote Wrightwick years afterwards, "he had neither the feeling of the Greek for simple majesty, nor that of the Roman for scenic grandeur, nor that of the Goth for picturesque effect, nor that of the schoolman for precedent; but, on the contrary, he seems to have taken from each a kind of negative hint, that operated in the production of a result, first showing that he had observed them, and *used* them, with a perfectly independent and exclusive regard for his own peculiar personal distinction."

A recluse in an age of cosmopolitan architecture; a meticulous deviser of things heretofore unseen in an era in which buildings were treasured for the facility with which they evoked precedent; a tender, sensitive if crotchety genius in an age which encouraged architectural entrepreneurs who could cobble their buildings out of historical prototypes like so many shoemakers, Soane was in dire need of a strong, light shell to protect himself and his work from the barbed criticisms of his contemporaries and from the ravages of time.

Soane's remains were buried beside those of his wife, in a vault beneath a commemorative monument that he fashioned in St. Pancras burial grounds in 1816, its flat-domed silhouette as personal in character as the interiors at Lincoln's Inn Fields. Together, his house and tomb represent, even if they do not totally comprise, the surviving fraction of the life work of the most profound and most necessarily eccentric English architect of his age.

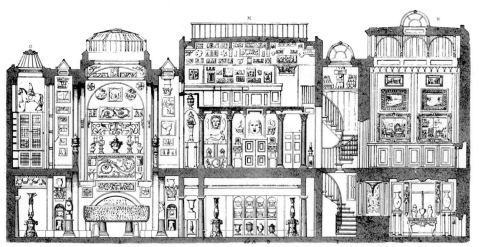

Section through the Museum, 1827; from *A New Description of Sir John Soane's Museum,* by John Summerson, 1955.

VIII

Fuseli, Blake, Palmer

By David Antin

Henry Fuseli

"There is living in Rome a noble German from Zurich, Henry Fuseli, a genius like a mountain torrent, a worshipper of Shakespeare, and now, Shakespeare's painter." [Johann Gottfried Herder, 1774]

"Shockingly mad, madder than ever, quite mad." [Horace Walpole, 1785]

"Fuseli's distortions and vagaries are German, and not English: they lie like a nightmare on the breast of our native art." [William Hazlitt, 1820]

"Estimate of Fuseli's work. Bizarre." [Johann Wolfgang von Goethe, 1797]

"Think of Fuseli's savage ferocity and abandoned women—the daughters of the bawds of hell, engendered by demons . . . Think of Fuseli's men—the sons of banditti . . . It can't be borne. The more I see of nature, the more I see of Raphael, the more I abhor Fuseli's mind, his subjects and his manner. Let me root his pictures from my fancy forever." [Benjamin Robert Haydon, 1812]

"A gentleman who visited me the other day said, 'I am very much surprised at the dislike that some connoisseurs show on viewing the pictures of Mr. Fuseli; but the truth is he is a hundred years beyond the present generation.' Though I am startled at such an assertion, I hope the contemporary taste will shorten the hundred years into as many hours, for I am sure that any person consulting his own eyes must prefer what is so supereminent." [William Blake, 1806]

Author

David Antin, poet, student of linguistics, editor of the little magazine *Some/Thing*, has written widely on painting as a form of communication.

William Blake: engraving after Fuseli's *Head of a Damned Man from Dante's Inferno,* 1790-92, 14 inches high [British Museum].

Fuseli always had a reputation as a bizarre painter, but among modern writers it is his admirers who find him bizarre. They tend to see him as a kind of proto-Surrealist, a visionary of "the dark chambers of the mind," a painter of "static horror." Generally these writers divide his work into two classes: the bulk of Fuseli's output, which they dismiss as "literary, mannered classicism," and a relatively smaller body of "dream pictures and twilight hallucinations," upon which his contemporary reputation is based. This is a distinction which Fuseli himself would never have made; and if one has no special bias for dreams, the works of the one category are just as bizarre as the other.

In a more or less ordinary early painting (dating between 1779 and 1781), an idealized young man in eighteenth century costume, one leg resting on a sofa, two fingers to his temple, sits listening to a witch or sorcerer in fur-trimmed robe and nightcap who is sitting beside him and admonishing him with a long bony finger. They are cloaked in secrecy by a drapery falling behind the young man's head and are brooded over by a great, blind-eyed face hovering above the table. It is not a scene out of opera. It is a perfectly common-place painting of the young Fuseli in conversation with Professor Bodmer. Bodmer was one of the leaders of the German *Sturm und Drang* avant-garde, the editor of the first modern edition of the Nibelungenlied and the Middle German romances. The subject of the conversation is poetry and the giant face above them is merely a bust of Homer (or some other blind man). The formula is apparent. The presence of the bust is intended simply to indicate that *the spirit of antique poetry* is present at the conversation. But something has gone wrong. Fuseli is not satisfied with the formula. Perhaps he feels it to be dead. He softens the stone of the bust till it no longer looks like marble, becomes more or less ectoplasmic, an apparition. It is almost a pun on the words *the spirit of antique poetry*. In the course of dissolution the features become acromegalic, Neanderthal. Bizarre.

Fuseli is above all a literary painter and literary in a very special way. He was largely self-taught. Though he was born into a family of painters he was compelled to enter the ministry, which he did apparently with no great strain. He fell in with the literary world of his native Zurich, where he was primarily known as a poet and translator to the German speaking world. It wasn't until 1770 that he decided to abandon literature for painting and at twenty-nine set off to study in Rome (apparently on the advice of Sir Joshua Reynolds, who is reported to have assured him on seeing a number of his sketches that a few years in Rome was all he needed to become "the world's greatest painter.") His period of study in Rome didn't come to much. He seems to have spent most of his eight years there reading and copying Renaissance masters and to have conceived a fatal passion for the works of Michelangelo. (According to Cunningham, in Rome Fuseli "affected the dress and mimicked the manners of Michael. . . . He loved to dream along the road—to follow the phantasies of an unbridled imagination—to pen sarcastic remarks—sketch colossal groups, and would call out ever and anon, when some strange thought struck him, 'Michelangelo!' ") When he reappeared in London in 1779 to set himself up as a professional painter at the age of 38 he arrived with a full baggage of fixed opinions and enthusiasms. He had a complete contempt for portraiture in the age of Reynolds and Gainsborough, despised landscape ("Strowger, bring me my umbrella, I am going to see Mr. Constable's pictures."), was indifferent to still-life, to genre, to all forms of the art that were not devoted to the "sublime" or "heroic." It is not surprising then that his works are primarily illustrations of scenes from the poetry he most admired, the plays of Shakespeare, the poems of Milton, Dante and Homer.

What are the subjects he selected? Lady Macbeth after the murder of Duncan, Macbeth with the Witches at the Cauldron, Titania and her fairy court, Hamlet and the Ghost, Lear renouncing Cordelia, Satan Bridging Chaos (from *Paradise Lost*), Paolo and Francesca, and Ugolino (from the *Divine Comedy*). The subjects are chosen because they represent the extremes of passion or of the marvelous, and the paintings are illustrations in a very particular sense. They are attempts to manifest the "emotions" inherent in the literary situation. To the degree that this is possible the paintings appear somewhat re-dundant. But usually it is not at all possible, even when the literary interpretation is adequate, because literary "emotions" are largely verbal and the relations between the verbal and the visual are arbitrary and conventional. Generally these conventional relation-ships are restricted to a very few elements of even the most representational paintings, e.g. gesture. Aside from these elements painting runs its own course. But Fuseli's literary concerns are so dominant that he tends to extend the domain of the literary to elements which are not conventionally dictated by literary choices such as color or space. When he is successful at this he can be called an all-over literary painter. This is usually what is meant by his "failure to render plastic values."

The most highly conventionalized verbal-visual relationships are human gestures. So it is only natural that Fuseli made the representation of the human figure the dominant element of his work. This involved him in a parasitic relation to theatrical convention, which both derives from and modifies human gesture. Moreover, he apparently felt that the musculature of the human body was in itself expressive of character and emotion, which explains his preference for the nude and his insistence that the art of ancient Greece was an art of "expression." In dealing with the human figure Fuseli employs certain visual formulas to convey the literary idea of the "sublime," which he interprets as a combination of "grandeur" and "terror." He renders "grandeur" by size (again almost a pun), both relative and absolute size, i.e. by the size of the figure in proportion to the other represented elements and by the actual size of the painting. (Unlike Blake he

Fuseli, Blake,
Palmer

had a strong concern for scale and was very bitter against "that Micromania which infects public taste.") He also employed characteristic deformations of the human body. To some extent these result from a merely obvious connection, e.g. massive shoulders equals "power," and his heroes occasionally look more like draft horses than men. It also results from a conventional misreading of Michelangelo, according to which the heavy, sagging flesh, which in fact projects nothing so much as an oppressively voluptuous fatigue, is interpreted as energy. Thanks to Fuseli's Neo-Classical taste for hard contours and smoothly modeled volumes, his painted figures look more like marble than flesh, and he invested them with "terror" by placing them in extreme theatrical attitudes and by propelling them into energetic motion. In particularly unfortunate examples, as in *Satan Taking His Flight from Chaos,* they look like flying gravestones.

From a contemporary point of view the most interesting aspect of Fuseli's work is his concern with the erotic. He is an erotic painter without being a voluptuous one. His hard line, his indifference to the Venetians, those great masters of pornography, contribute to the apparent coldbloodedness of his erotic paintings: but there is also a satirical element that must not be overlooked. This is very marked in paintings like the *Nightmare,* where a horse's head is thrust squarely into the center of the painting, or the *Incubus* where a horse's rump is displayed conspicuously as the two nude women in the disarrayed bed stare stupidly into space, and in the moronic donkey face of Bottom in the painting from *A Midsummer Night's Dream.* This malicious concentration on the stupefying aspects of passion is not consistent with a simple romantic attitude to extremes of feeling. The horse's head in *Nightmare* is a punning retort to romantic passion. Fuseli is very Freudian in dealing with suppressed sexual desire, which invades the dream in the form of stupid demons. He also shares this attitude to sexual suppression with Blake. But unlike Blake, Fuseli treats all erotic situations as scenes of stupid lust. The point of view of his erotic work is that of the satirist or voyeur. At his best, in this cold fascination with the erotic-ridiculous projected by his caricaturist's line and skillful washes, his drawings bear comparison to Daumier's.

Blake

"Fuseli called on me last night and sat till 12 o'clock. He mentioned Blake, the Engraver, whose genius and invention have been much spoken of. Fuseli has known him several years and thinks he has a great deal of invention, but that fancy is the end and not a means in his designs. He does not employ it to give novelty and decoration to regular

William Blake: *Nebuchadnezzar,* 1795, watercolor heightened with pen and ink, 17 inches high, an enlarged version of a subject in Blake's illuminated book, *The Marriage of Heaven and Hell,* interpreting the line "One law for the Lion and Ox is Oppression" (Minneapolis Art Institute).

111

conceptions, but the whole of his aim is to produce singular shapes and odd combinations."
[Farington Diary, 1796]

In 1796 "Blake, the Engraver," was thirty-nine years old. He had completed the *Songs of Innocence and Experience, The Visions of the Daughters of Albion, The Marriage of Heaven and Hell* and all of the shorter prophetical books. He was the most exciting poet in England, perhaps in all Europe. The ideas behind *The Marriage of Heaven and Hell* should have started a literary revolution or at least got him locked up for sedition. But nobody read them. No more than nine copies of *The Marriage* and no more than seventeen of *The Visions* were printed in his lifetime. He was the greatest controversialist of the age and he had nobody to fight with. When he finally did get tried for sedition the circumstances were farcical. A quarrelsome soldier intruded into Blake's garden and subsequently trumped up marvelously accurate slanders in revenge for being forcibly ejected by the poet. The only consequence of the entire affair was that the soldier got his name into Blake's unread epic *Jerusalem* as a minor demon.

As a painter Blake was not much better known. He had been exhibiting his "designs" (primarily drawings and watercolors) at the Royal Academy since 1780, and though they were "spoken of," he was still "Blake, the Engraver." But this requires some qualification. The most impressive of Blake's designs to this point had been printed in his own illuminated books; and since these were unread, the best of his work was largely unknown. And when it was known it was generally misunderstood. Thus Fuseli: "he does not employ it [his invention] to give novelty and decoration to regular conceptions." Blake probably never had a "regular conception" in his life, and what is more he had his own conceptions (irregular?) of almost every issue that concerned his age.

Blake was if anything a more literary painter than Fuseli, but he was literary in a different way. For Blake, his poetry and painting were two complementary means of expounding his "conceptions" or "visions." And in this sense he is not an illustrator of his own or anyone else's poetry. This is clearest when his apparent task is to illustrate some well known literary work. Even a superficial glance at his illustrations for *The Book of Job,* Homer or Dante reveals that Blake uses the text as an occasion for expounding his vision. His conceptions of *The Laocoon Group* (engraved about 1820) are characteristic and far from "regular." The title printed on the engraving reads "Jehovah & his two Sons, Satan & Adam, as they were copied from the Cherubim of Solomon's Temple and applied to Natural Fact, or the History of Ilium." The central figure in the group is labeled "The Angel of the Divine Presence," and below in Hebrew, "Angel of Jehovah," and in Greek below this, "The Serpent Bearer." The serpent on the right is labeled "Evil," and the one on the left "Good" and "Lilith." This allegorical treatment of classical texts is typical, but Blake is almost as free with his own poems. The last plate of

Fuseli, Blake Palmer

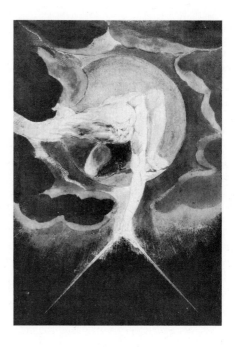

William Blake: a watercolor drawing for Milton's *Paradise Lost*: *Adam and Eve Sleeping* [left], ca. 1808 [Boston Museum]. Milton's work occupied a very significant place in Blake's imagination and fed into his poem *Milton* (1800-04). Blake thought of him as a poet of partially obscured vision, to be corrected by himself.

William Blake: an illumination from *Jerusalem,* which was not completed before 1818: *Los at the foot of the Tree of Crucifixion* [near right; National Gallery, Washington, D. C.]; and the watercolor frontispiece to *Europe: a Prophecy,* printed in 1794: *The Ancient of Days Setting a Dividers on the Face of the Earth* [far right; Philadelphia Museum].

The Marriage of Heaven and Hell is illustrated with the figure of Nebuchadnezzar, who is never once mentioned in the poem; and the forty-second plate of *Milton* is a picture drawn from the text of plate 94 of *Jerusalem,* with which it has no apparent connection. In this sense Blake's designs are no more illustrations of the texts than the texts are illustrations of the pictures. They are equivalent, complementary and sometimes deliberately contradictory images of Blake's vision. Which makes them terribly difficult to deal with—not only because the iconography is sometimes obscure, but because even when this is clear it is not certain whether or not a given picture is intended to be funny. The troll-like figures of Urizen (the *Book of Urizen*) and the pussy-cat Tyger (of the *Songs*) are cases in point. To understand the individual images of both the pictures and poems it is necessary to understand the whole vision.

The vision as a whole is not difficult to understand, but at the same time it is easy to see why it was totally unacceptable to his contemporaries. Blake had been expounding it from 1788 and the general outline is exceptionally clear. Blake despised the politics, morality and religion of his day and he was a thorough going anti-supernaturalist. In this he was with all the radicals of his day. But it is one thing to say that there is no God except in the mind of man—an argument with which all his radical friends could agree—and another to follow this up with: we must therefore explore man's mind in order to find God. The conclusion to *There is no Natural Religion,* "God becomes as we are, that we may be as he is," is nothing other than the commonplace naturalist aphorism "Man makes God in his own image." But for Blake the perfectly logical consequences of this conclusion are two questions that form the remainder of his work: then how did we come to this terrible state of affairs and how can we redeem both man and God? But here he was all alone. From the orthodox, for whom he had little use in any event, he had parted company at the first axiom, from the radicals at the first inference. From here on Blake became a kind of allegorical psychologist rather like Buber or Jung. The *Visions of the Daughters of Albion* begins the assault on false morality, which in *The Marriage* escalates into an assault on false religion that in the name of reason polarizes being into "good" and "evil." The *Proverbs of Hell* sound as if they might have been written by a more intelligent Sade:

Prudence is a rich ugly old maid courted by Incapacity.
He who desires but acts not, breeds pestilence.
The cut worm forgives the plow.
Dip him in the river who loves water.

If the fool would persist in his folly he would become wise.

The pride of the peacock is the glory of God.
The lust of the goat is the bounty of God.
The wrath of the lion is the wisdom of God.
The nakedness of woman is the work of God.

You never know what is enough unless you know what is more than enough.

Exuberance is beauty.
Sooner murder an infant in its cradle than nurse unacted desires.

Enough! or too much.

It is here also we get the clearest picture of his attitude to the figures of his mythology. And Blake on occasion plays very whimsically with them ("I have always found that Angels have the vanity to speak of themselves as the only wise; this they do with a confident insolence sprouting from systematic reasoning.") Too much has been made of the figures Blake saw in his visions, of their metaphysical status, of the nature of his belief in them. That he could take them seriously is fairly obvious. After all he wrote about them all of his life and they were an intrinsic part of his vocabulary ("I am not ashamed or averse to tell You what you Ought to be Told: That I am under the direction of Messengers from Heaven, Daily & Nightly . . ."). But he was also not above a put-on, like the description of a fairy's funeral for a credulous lady or accommodating fictions like the tedious descriptions of the great dead for his dull-witted astrologer friend Varley. Still, the most significant statement he made about visions occurs in his interrogation of the prophets Isaiah and Ezekiel in *The Marriage*: "The prophets Isaiah and Ezekiel dined with me, and I asked them how they dared so roundly assert that God spoke to

Fuseli, Blake
Palmer

William Blake: illustration for a passage in *Revelation* xii: "a woman clothed with the sun, and the moon under her feet . . . and behold a great red dragon"; probably dating from 1805-10, as most of his watercolors [National Gallery, Washington, D. C.].

them; and whether they did not think at the time that they would be misunderstood, & so be the cause of imposition, Isaiah answered: 'I saw no God, nor heard any, in any finite organical perception; but my senses discovered the infinite in everything, and as I was then perswaded, & remain confirmed, that the voice of honest indignation is the voice of God, I cared not for consequences but wrote.' "

If Blake followed Isaiah's literary program then the rest of his career can be seen as nothing more nor less than an allegorical analysis of man's fall from "Poetical Genius," his initially divine state, into his present catastrophic condition and a scheme for his renovation. The tactics are implicit in the words *the fall*. Blake's demonology becomes an attempt to reinterpret *The Fall of Man* as a precipitation from wholeness into a narrow, rational and fearful selfhood; renovation is achieved at the end of *Jerusalem* by annihilation of this self. Blake's thorough realization that his demons were mere masks for deceptive psychological states put him in an equivocal position as an artist. How to accommodate visually a figure of speech that verbally can run the range from demon to child of light as in the letter to Hayley: "O Glory! and O Delight! I have entirely reduced that spectrous fiend to his station, whose annoyance has been in the ruin of my labours for the last passed 20 years of my life. He is the enemy of conjugal love, and is the Jupiter of the Greeks, an iron hearted tyrant, the ruiner of ancient Greece. I speak with perfect confidence and certainty of the fact which has passed upon me. Nebuchadnezzar has seven times passed over him; I have had 20; thank God I was not altogether a beast as he was; but I was a slave bound in a mill among beasts and devils; these beasts and devils are now, together with myself, become children of light and liberty."

Frequently Blake's solution took the form of pictorial comedy. The absurd-looking figures of the Blake mythology are deliberate parodies of the mental states represented. Comically ferocious demons give way to comically pathetic ones. The pathetic Urizen and the absurd Nebuchadnezzar are typical Blakean solutions. In other instances, as in the illustrations to *The Book of Job* and the *Arlington Court Regeneration Picture,* Blake resorted to a schematic separation of reality levels. The effect of this tactic is anti-dramatic, and it gives the pictures a more or less heraldic character, the significance of which could only be grasped by someone thoroughly acquainted with Blake's over-all conceptions, which were by no means "regular." What is more, Blake's artistic intentions are further obscured by his complete lack of sensitivity to pictorial scale. The poems, in Blake's own words, have as their subjects "Giants," yet the paintings regardless of subject must inevitably fit within the modest dimensions of the page. Regardless of its quality it is almost impossible for a book illustration, which is not likely to exceed in size one sixth the magnitude of the human body, to convey an impression of the "titanic."

Blake's painting not only does not illustrate his work, in the sense of making it clearer, but increases the difficulty of understanding it. Given the urgency of Blake's polemical

Fuseli, Blake, Palmer

William Blake: a sketch from *Jerusalem*: *Time's Triple Bow* [left], pencil drawing, 12½ inches high [National Gallery, Washington, D. C.].

Samuel Palmer's "romance with transitional states of light . . . not very far from the Impressionist romance with sunlight": *Cornfield by Moonlight with Evening Star* [right], ca. 1830, watercolor, gouache and ink, 7¾ inches high [Collection Sir Kenneth Clark, Kent].

William Blake: *Newton*, 1795, watercolor drawing, 17½ inches high [Tate Gallery, London]. Newton is not the "scientist" Newton, but an "angelic" figure in Blake's pantheon and related to the Ancient of Days in an unfallen state.

Blake: illustration to Dante's *Inferno: The Simoniac Pope,* 1824-27, watercolor, 20½ inches high [Tate Gallery, London].

Samuel Palmer: *A Hilly Scene,* ca. 1826, watercolor, ink and tempera, heavily varnished, on panel, 8½ inches high [Tate Gallery, London].

Henry Fuseli: illustration for Wieland's epic poem *Oberon:*
Huon Freeing Babekan Attacked by a Lion, 1804, 24½ inches high.
This colorplate is taken from Gert Schiff's forthcoming catalogue
raisonné of Fuseli to be published by the Schweizerisches Institut fur
Kunstwissenschaft, Zurich, which promises to be definitive.

to have worked in the free English watercolor style after the Fielding brothers, Bonington and Turner. But John Linnell introduced him to the work of the Dutch landscapists and to the already elderly Blake. These encounters were decisive. Though his work doesn't resemble either Blake's or the Dutch landscape school, it is easy to see the derivations from both. Blake is responsible for at least two elements in Palmer's work, chiefly a reinforcement of the idea of the "poetic," which was probably not very strong or original in Palmer. For Palmer this idea took obvious shape in certain emblems in Blake's woodcuts for Thornton's *Virgil*. In Palmer's Shoreham works there are literal quotations of Blake's crescent moon "bearing the old moon in its arms," the backlightings with the rising sun, the muscular, elmlike tree centered in the foreground. Blake with his engraver's tradition also reinforced Palmer's predilection for hard line as surface pattern. But Palmer absorbed these elements on his own terms. His sense of space is much surer than Blake's. In his major works Blake was not much concerned with illusory space. Blake's is the sporadic space of the illuminated manuscripts or heraldic devices. Palmer is always a landscapist who can suggest atmospheric space with line, the great trick of the Dutch landscape drawings. His ability to combine the Dutch quasi-realist tradition and Blake's neo-Gothic is incredible. It is accomplished mainly by lighting. Sharp alternations of dark and light masses which are encountered in nature only when the light source is relatively low in the sky, at twilight or sunrise, or when the light source is relatively weak, as in moonlight, allow Palmer sharp compressions of the picture space. At the same time the uncertain reflections create sharp, unnatural linear patterns by depriving objects of most of their mass. The abstract handling of the wheat in *Cornfield by Moonlight* is typical. The over-all concern is the romance with transitional states of light—this is clear from his Notebooks —the poetical commonplaces "twilight," "sunrise" and "moonlight." It is not very far from this to the Impressionist romance with sunlight or van Gogh's.

But for some reason, sometime after 1832 Palmer turned from the Shoreham landscapes to Claude's Italian ones. Technically it was not immensely different. Claude also has the low backlighting, sharp light and dark masses, though the space is deeper and the abstract line is missing. Visually it was all the difference in the world. There is no way of accounting for the change. For if Shoreham's landscapes bored him, at least he had invented them. Claude's were boring before Palmer was born. A way out appeared in *Plantation*, where sharply outlined objects coexist in a kind of hallucinatory brilliance, but he reverted to placid Italian landscapes, until he died in 1881.

Fuseli, Blake, Palmer

Henry Fuseli: *The Nightmare,* 40 inches high [Detroit Institute of Arts]. There are a number of versions of this theme dating from as early as 1781.

IX

The Imprint of Hercules Seghers

By Charles James Wright

Author:

Charles James Wright is an artist and Professor of Painting at the Allen R. Hite Art Institute of the University of Louisville, Kentucky. In his own engravings he has experimented with techniques first used by Seghers.

One of Hercules Seghers' characteristic, haunting night scenes, *The Ruin with Bushes*. Dark blue paint was applied to the finished etching to enhance the nocturnal effect. Here, as elsewhere in Seghers' œuvre, the Roman look of the ruins has led to speculation that the artist actually visited Italy. (Unless otherwise noted, all works of Seghers in this article are in the collection of the Rijksprentenkabinet in Amsterdam).

Eccentricity is a relative term in the arts in the sense that all creative effort of the highest quality must exist apart from the mainstream. "Different" might describe better an art which, in theory at least, is out of step with trends, or which by its innate structure finds itself isolated from the art which is considered acceptable at a given time. Art pays honor exclusively to its own image or language. Great artists, like all great men, are isolated, and not demoralized by this fact. They dare. They invent. After the facts of creation, they sometimes judge; not before. And very likely the greatest artists never judge their work from the eccentric point of view. Great inventiveness results, it would seem, in great art—assuming that either immediately (which is unlikely), or in time, the general public will catch up.

Hercules Seghers' fascination or obsession with the techniques of print-making was endless. This, if nothing else, made his approach to the art seem unique. He was the first print-maker to understand that a print could become a much greater statement than a simple ink impression upon a sheet of paper, and that if it were properly explored it could result in an art more closely akin to painting. He improvised and with incredible deftness sought and found a myriad of new printed effects. His use of colored inks—many of which he must have made himself—was a preliminary step toward richer intaglio prints. Then, once he had matched his complementary combinations (reds and blues, greens and oranges, yellows and blues), he began to explore and experiment with colored paper and cloth. How simple it appears to express the shimmering mystery of a night scene! But to express such an impression in concrete graphic terms is an astounding achievement, and to have done so in the early seventeenth century, when the art of etching had been moribund in Europe for generations, was even more astounding. With no precedents, Seghers aspired to such visualization and even today we are taken aback by his masterful results. The blue-black of night is broken by the pale yellow-white intaglio line of moonlight sparkling over the ruins of an abbey, a bush or a wall. He proofed, counter-proofed and then transposed prints from paper to linen. Such experiments in colored intaglio prints were his methods in a search to give form to his vision. With these techniques, and by accepting workshop accidents during the process of print-making, the artist transformed "happenings" into personal visions. The results can become either great works of art or nothing more than clever tricks. Seghers, using brush and pen, with the classic tools (burin and needle) for marking the prepared plate, freed himself from the restrictions imposed by a limiting, traditional technique.

In the peaceful, prosperous Holland of the early seventeenth century, painting tended generally to celebrate people, prosperity, wealth and other more or less rational adjuncts to the factual imagination. Seghers departed from this tradition. Although his forms remained essentially classical (created by the use of light gradations from black to white), his concepts in the use of form, the meaning of form and the *totality* of form were shocking. He was not a simple realist; a Seghers landscape was not meant as a portrayal of some

Two Trees in Leaf [above] may have been influenced by Chinese porcelain, which had begun to reach Holland.

Characteristic use of a foreground tree and plateau to give remoteness to a distant peak: *The Rocky Landscape* [below].

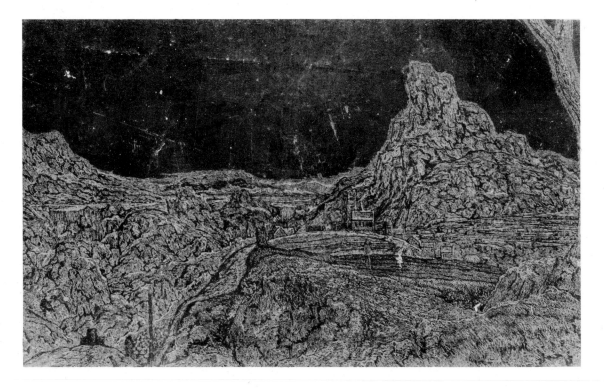

One of two known etchings by Seghers
showing a storm at sea [above], *Ship in a
Rough Sea* is printed in yellow on brown.

The fantastic detail of its foliage and
knotted bark confers a curious
kind of life on *The Big Tree* [below].

local scene. In some ways he looks back toward the "world landscape" of the sixteenth century, that is, a landscape which could exist anywhere or everywhere, although at the same time his generalized landscapes seem made up of real, particularized elements. Often his interpretation of a simple natural subject like a tree became an enormously intricate network of color, line and technique, until the final tree-like statement seems to embody the elements of all trees. Nature for Seghers was no idle accessory to the human condition. The simplest rock formation was an enormous totality. A mountain was not merely a topological phenomenon but also a magnificent mass of line and color, of weight and form, of matter and spirit.

Curiously, the elaborate handling of a simple natural motif is reversed when he treats complicated ones. Raging seas, wind-tossed ships and brooding skies fuse into vivid, but simple, representations. One might generalize and say that Seghers complicated simple natural images and simplified complicated ones. In this sense he could be considered something of an abstractionist. In addition he frequently broke with tradition, as it had been understood, by using unnatural combinations of objects. Who in early seventeenth-century Holland would have had the odd idea of placing windmills on the tops of mountains or Greek temples in the Dutch countryside? These seeming absurdities confuse historians, but in view of Seghers' basic premise of total commitment, why couldn't a Classical temple spring up in Holland as well as in Greece? Couldn't a windmill be erected atop a mountain? Where better to expose it to the workings and wanderings of the wind? Hence, even in his absurdities, we detect proofs of a higher logic. Similarly, in some of his prints we notice interlaced pathways which do not appear to "start" or "arrive" anywhere; which wander strangely in, out, over, around. Once again we are forced to admit that such pathways are not intended as local roads, but to represent the universality of all avenues. The artist understands that such an answer is general, if not downright vague.

Seghers himself was reserved about his techniques, and, contrary to the usual practice of the period, he was not known to have engaged apprentices. Thus most of his processes have long remained a mystery. Evidence now slowly being unearthed suggests that he used many soft-ground substances which could be easily scraped or rubbed away depending on the effects sought. He experimented widely with broad fluid line techniques, the acid slowly breaking down the plates, and finally with elaborate applications of liquid grounds.

His style remained much the same throughout his career and the long accumulation of his work. Whether or not a style actually helps to establish an artist remains debatable,

The Imprint of Hercules Seghers

This magnificent painting in the Boymans Museum in Rotterdam shows Seghers' gift for abstracting the particulars of a landscape. The trees in the detail [right] prove that he was a keen observer of nature, yet *Landscape* as a whole [below] has a "world-landscape" feel.

Little but the windmill in the quasi-abstract *Landscape with a Windmill* [above] can be identified specifically.

Probably an imaginary scene, *Town with Four Towers* [below] mingles Dutch and Italianate architectural styles.

Notable for its curious pointillist
technique, *Castle with Two High Towers*
[above] may be Stahleck, near Bacharach.

An incomplete impression of *Rocky River
Landscape with Mountain Road* [below].
Another greatly altered version exists.

Three of some 15 known versions of *Landscape with Waterfall*. Seghers worked over the proofs with the dry point, and in some versions added oil colors. The teeming, "lunar" aspect of the landscape and the absence of people in this seemingly inhabited region add a note of mystery.

for if concentrated effort is directed toward its formulation, quality seems to suffer. On the other hand, lack of identifiable style weakens an artist's identity. In the case of Seghers, it is reasonable to suspect that his style was a combination of both image and method. From a purely technical point of view, his work is readily identified by its nervous, worm-like, wiggling lines, a device which enabled him both to capture the fleeting look of foliage, clouds and water, and to indulge his predilection for swarming detail. He did not hesitate to overstep the limits of printmaking, for instance by such "modern" methods as treating the finished print with special combinations of varnish or even oil colors. Such techniques can produce almost surreal effects, and the resemblance of his more fantastic landscapes to Max Ernst's *frottages* has often been noted.

Seghers' work did not achieve even modest attention until the late nineteenth and early twentieth centuries, although, as Leo C. Collins points out in his book on the master, "a certain tradition of collecting prints by Seghers, although not uninterrupted, can be traced from the seventeenth century to our day," and outstanding examples of his work from former private collections can be found in the Rijksprentenkabinet in Amsterdam, the Albertina, the Bibliothèque Nationale and the British Museum, among others. His paintings did not fare so well: barely a century ago no painting by him was known, the first to be identified being the *Great Mountain View* in the Uffizi which, like many other Seghers works, had previously been attributed to Rembrandt.

The Imprint of Hercules Seghers

Seghers was probably born in 1589, and died about 1638. Most of his life was spent in Haarlem, Amsterdam and The Hague. He studied in Amsterdam with the landscape painter Gilles van Coninxloo (d. 1606), and is mentioned in the membership rolls of the Guild of St. Luke in Haarlem in 1612. He appears to have married twice, and to have enjoyed a period of affluence during which he bought a fine house in Amsterdam, which he later sold at a loss. Little is known of his travels beyond the evidence of a painted view of Brussels, but it has been generally supposed that he made the traditional trip to Italy; certainly the Italianate character of some of his landscapes suggests it, as does the influence of the style and engraving technique of Adam Elsheimer, who was living in Rome when Seghers was a young man.

It is to be hoped that more biographical details may one day come to light, but the lack of them in no way hinders our appreciation of Seghers as one of the greatest graphic artists who ever lived. In the recent international revival of print-making, he has come to be recognized as one of the fathers of modern engraving, for his inspired technical innovations and for his haunting, visionary overtones. Both contribute to make him, in Walter Pater's famous definition, "a seeker after something in the world that is there in no satisfying measure, or not at all."

One of a handful of surviving drawings by Seghers is the wraithlike *Farmhouse with a Man Sitting on a Fence.*

134

X

Nineteenth-Century Eccentrics and the American Tradition

By William C. Agee

Author

William C. Agee is Associate Curator at the Whitney Museum. Formerly he worked at the Archives of American Art.

Dead Soldier, drawing, by William Rimmer (1816-1879), who taught anatomy and is best known for his allegorical sculpture. The telescoped view is emblematic of the facts of life and death— the hand thrust against the frame, a glimpse of anguish [Boston Museum].

Writing to the poet Henry Pickering in 1827, Washington Allston referred to Thomas Cole by saying: "He has chosen a profession in itself innocent, and if properly pursued— that is, for its own sake—in a high degree elevating. Indeed it seems as if no one could truly love nature without loving its divine author, who in all His works, even in the horrible, no less than in the beautiful, speaks only in the language of love." To a great extent this sense of innocence which has characterized our people and so much of our art may account for the scarcity of truly eccentric American painters. Only Albert Ryder, William Rimmer, John Quidor and Ralph Blakelock produced an art that was fully and consistently eccentric. Beyond them there are single paintings scattered at random through the œuvres of disparate and otherwise wholly conventional artists to be considered. These sporadic works, however, are more than passing curiosities or minor and uncharacteristic examples of an artist's style; they are intrinsic to his sensibility, and reveal a latent imagination caught in a dichotomy created by the very special circumstances of the nineteenth-century milieu. The innocence to which Allston referred can be traced to the American artist's detachment from the long European tradition of what Robert Motherwell has called the sense of our alien past. That past and its common forces of violence, guilt and mystery, the psychic stuff of which the eccentric vision is made, were far removed from the freshness of a new world where, as Cole said, "all nature is new to art." The promise of the new could only submerge deeper impulses that might seek to explore the dark recesses of the mind.

The American artist who wished to dream and create in mystic realms found himself severely hampered by a public that valued only the literal, the tangible and the useful. Copley's lament that the artist was considered no more than a tradesman, or Cole's indictment of a society in which "the tide of utility sets against the fine arts," are but two incidents in a sad and all-too-familiar story. But the dichotomy evident in the random manifestations of the eccentric vision can also be traced to the artist's ambivalent attitude to the country. All through our history, despite his protests against the vulgarity, philistinism and insensitivity of public, collector and patron alike, the artist has been fascinated and captivated by the pace and texture of American life. While rebelling, he has caught at the same time its infectious spirit, which has in turn provided a compelling pictorial energy. If at times it was in spite of himself, the artist has sought to portray the sweep of the American panorama, to come to grips with and capture its special quality. It has been an elusive search and, as John McCoubrey has rightly observed, has often meant a confusion between an American subject matter and an American style. Above all, it has meant a persistent strain of realism and a frank acceptance of life as it is. Whether it be in the rural scenes of Mount, Bingham, Homer, Benton or Curry, or the urban images of

Krimmel, Henri, Marsh, Davis, Sheeler or Rosenquist, the artist has faced America head-on. His cheerful acceptance and celebration of the rawness of this country is equally reflected in W. MacKay Laffan's proclamation of 1880, "There be more joy over one honest and sincere American horse pond, over one truthful and dirty tenement, over one unaffected sugar refinery, over one vulgar but unostentatious coal wharf than there shall be over nine and ninety mosques of St. Sophia," and Franz Kline's, "Half the world spends its life at Walden trying to escape the traffic to Boston. The other half is part of that traffic. We like the second half. Right?"

The lasting effect of this preoccupation has been to shift the artist's eye outward to an empirically accessible reality rather than to an interior world of private fantasy. The eccentric has appeared, even if only momentarily, when he has turned away from the pictorial abundance of the country. He has seen neither the material splendors nor shared the moral certitudes of a boundless optimism in the future. He has dwelled, often with a quiet nostalgia for a lost paradise, in a veiled world of the undefined and enigmatic. As if to recapture a distantly remembered past, his pictorial stage was often one on which time and movement are suspended, as if in a muted, dream-like world. We can count as a result very little painting that is of the utterly fantastic, bizarre or grotesque sort that we associate with Blake, Fuseli and Redon. Even amid scenes of overt violence one feels not the psychopathic fever of a nightmare, but what de Tocqueville described as "the

Nineteenth-Century Eccentrics and the American Tradition

Cole's *Titan's Goblet* [right], 1833, is perhaps his symbol of a Druidic Tree of Life [19 inches high; Metropolitan Museum, New York].

Thomas Cole's image of life as the *Architect's Dream* [bottom; detail left], 1840, may represent an ideal world of peace and order, but there is also an air of impending destruction [54 inches high; Toledo Museum].

strange melancholy which often haunts inhabitants of democratic countries and disgust at life that seizes them in the midst of calm and easy circumstances."

The eccentric in America remained detached and remote to an even greater extent than his European counterpart. For the most part he worked very quietly within the contours of the Romantic and Symbolist movements and, with the lone exception of Ryder, effected no visible impact on later art. That much of our eccentric painting has emerged at random and at unlikely points as the work of artists who do not tower over their generations is a cause of some difficulty in defining just who might be considered truly eccentric. To thus term Thomas Cole, William Page and Thomas Dewing as eccentric on the basis of one or two paintings may seem wholly arbitrary when others with ostensible similarities are excluded. But that which distinguishes the true eccentric, and engages our interest, is that his special way of seeing is essentially without precedent. In some cases, such as Field or Quidor, he remains entirely removed from any identifiable pictorial currents. In others, such as Ryder, Cole or Newman, we recognize that his vision foreshadows new and viable modes of exploring the artistic consciousness, and demonstrates what can be admitted to the domain of the artist's vocabulary. Because he thus looks ahead to the beginning of something, rather than to the end of a tradition, we begin to perceive the roots of a modern outlook. In his apartness, in his turn from the world of appearances, the eccentric recognized the essential contingency of the human condition; he was thus led to probe the deepest impulses and aspirations of the self, and in this search we find the seeds of modern thought. This is not to attempt to cast a bogus legitimization on these paintings; nor is it to read them out of context by imposing purely twentieth-century values on them, a distortion of the kind found in the connection between Magic Realism and Harnett, Peto and Haberle. These three are part of a living American tradition and are here excluded, as are Vedder, LaFarge, the Beards and Church, all of whom—although in some respects curious—are understandable in the context of their times.

The problem of inclusion is further clouded by instances of pure accident or coincidence which, despite their intent, may well be truly eccentric. For example, Martin Heade's painting, *Gremlins in the Studio* (collection Irving Burton, Detroit) was started as a landscape of wooded marshland, a motif which Heade frequently employed. However, when it was about three-quarters finished, Heade left the studio; his good friend Frederic Church entered and finished the painting as a practical joke. He added a platform on supports to hold the landscape. Over it water spills and beneath, a globe-headed urchin dances in merriment. Only a joke to be sure, but the visual pun, the irony and association of dissimilar elements offers an image worthy of Miró or Ernst. It is not the nineteenth-century view of nature as an exalted and purifying presence, but a shallow stage prop.

As another instance, how is one to consider the famous *Staircase Group* by Charles

Nineteenth-Century
Eccentrics and
the American Tradition

An eccentric picture or a practical joke?
M. J. Heade's *Gremlins in the Studio,* ca. 1870
[10 inches high; collection Irving Burton,
Detroit] started as a landscape, but
was finished by Heade's friend, the painter
Frederic Church, who added the sawhorses,
the globe-headed urchin and made the water
overflow to the floor. The gesture also
implies a question to Heade's idealist
nature-worship. The title was given later.

James Hamilton: *The Last Days of Pompeii* [detail], 1864,
63³⁄₁₆ inches high. Bulwer-Lytton's novel serves as a
pretext for a holocaust alluding to the Day of Judgment
by this artist better known for factual marinescapes
[collection of David Orr; colorplate Brooklyn Museum].

Willson Peale? When the painting, which depicted Peale's two sons on a staircase, was exhibited at the Columbianum Exhibition of 1795, a wooden stairwell was built out from the picture frame to complete an illusion so convincing that George Washington is said to have been deceived. Is this only an early example of an extreme trompe-l'œil, or is it a visionary forecast of a continuing American concern for narrowing the distinction between painting and sculpture, between "art" and "life," reality and illusion, that has marked the twentieth-century?

As the first American in whom the dichotomy between the world of natural fact and private fantasy can be discerned, Thomas Cole (1801-1848) found himself continually torn between the public demand for his landscapes and his imaginative impulses. His allegorical series of the *Voyage of Life* and *Course of Empire* expressed the deep-seated Romantic themes of change, the passage of time and the mutability of "earthly things" which had been shaped to a great extent by Volney's influential work, *Ruins, or Meditations on the Revolutions of Empires.* But for his truly extraordinary *Titan's Goblet,* no such readily apparent motivations are forthcoming. It is said to have been based on a Norse legend of the Tree of Life, but that interpretation is far from certain. The double image of tree as goblet, an irrational association which was later a standard Surrealist device, invokes a world of the dream, floating, suspended and suddenly glimpsed as in a moment of awakening. The image of life as a dream, more explicit in the *Architect's Dream* (1840, Toledo Museum), may represent an ideal and primeval world of infinite peace and order, but they may both imply an impending destruction, for Cole's stilled world of the subconscious remains an enigmatic and perplexing venture into the unknown, the ephemeral and the unreal.

Far from Cole's silent enigmas, John Quidor (1801-1881) came close to realizing an art of the fantastic and bizarre; only a degree of humor and caricature stopped him short. Nevertheless Quidor evolved a painting of emotional intensity rare in its time. Virtually unknown in his day and still too little appreciated, Quidor was most successful in giving a visual animation to Washington Irving's *Sketch Book* and *Tales of a Traveler.* He was born in Tappan, N.Y. and came to New York City where he studied briefly with John Wesley Jarvis. Traces of Dutch genre, Hogarth and Rowlandson can be found in his style after 1830, but at his best Quidor presented a unique blend of the Gothic and the narrative. His interest stems not only from the weird and fanciful characterizations of Irving's protagonists but from the projection of their emotions into the inanimate objects of their surroundings. *The Money Diggers,* 1832, is based on a passage from *Tales of a Traveler* in which the ghostly apparition of the drowned buccaneer was spotted by those who had unearthed his chest of gold, and which ends, "All was horror and confusion." The fright of their recognition is clear enough, but what generates the electric intensity of the scene is the anthropomorphic gyrations of the trees, rocks and earth. The sense of supernatural presence that also reigns in the *Tom Walker* series ca. 1856, is as much due to the highly charged atmosphere as it is to Quidor's figure of the devil. More than just an illustrator of a rich native literature, Quidor achieved an extension of human emotion in his distorted and exaggerated pictorial forms. These expressive distortions represent an intensity of rhythm, line and color not attempted again until Ryder.

James Hamilton (1819-1878), long known as the "American Turner," was essentially a painter of the sea. Very few of his works can be called eccentric, but among those that are we can count images of almost Biblical proportions. Hamilton had come from his native Ireland at an early age to Philadelphia where he began to study art. His admiration for Turner was soon evident, and his epic paintings of the sea earned him a considerable reputation by 1850. He was a restless traveler, both literally and vicariously, having gone to England and across the United States, and in 1854, fascinated by Elisha Kent Kane's journeys to the Arctic, Hamilton translated Kane's sketches into a series of memorable paintings. His style always tended to a tight, linear precision, but during the years 1855-70, a broader, more painterly manner was introduced. Both manners could accommodate Hamilton's flights of imagination. *The Vision of Columbus,* painted in 1850 with graphic detail, shows the explorer's three boats sailing into a low horizon, while emerging from the clouds and moving across the sky is a long column of figures. Some are winged, some appear armed, as if they were the warriors of the Lord, revealing themselves in triumphal procession. The sense of a personal revelation, of a hallucinatory vision was dramatically climaxed by Hamilton in his masterpiece, *The Last Days of Pompeii.* Bulwer's novel serves as a pretext for a coloristic holocaust in which the heavens, more than a volcano,

John Quidor's *The Money Diggers* [above], 1832 [16¾ inches high; Brooklyn Museum], and *The Devil and Tom Walker* [below], 1856 [27 inches high; collection of Mr. and Mrs. Lawrence A. Fleischman, New York], both based on incidents in Washington Irving's *Tales of a Traveler.* In the first, treasure seekers come upon the ghost of a drowned buccaneer guarding his chest of gold; in the second, Tom Walker uncovers a skull cloven by a tomahawk and is warned off by the Devil. Quidor did not merely illustrate but drew on literary subjects for his intensely imaginative scenes.

open and pour forth destruction below. Pompeii may be a symbol of modern civilization about to face its day of Judgment, for Hamilton's explosive bursts of color, amid which appears what might be taken for the statue of the Redeemer, create an apocalyptic fury. Hamilton's inferno, issuing a warning of terrible finality, takes us into a vortex of creation.

Although some of his work now seems strange and brooding, William Page did only one painting which might truly be considered eccentric. He was the sort of man who might have been expected to produce more, for his mind was continually seeking the unusual. Born in Albany, he had come to New York in 1820; there he studied with Samuel F. B. Morse, but then decided to prepare for the ministry. He studied theology for two years before returning to art. He had gone to Italy in 1849, where Powers introduced him to the ideas of Swedenborg, which preoccupied him in the later part of his life. Page's thinking was frequently confused, but the unpredictable nature of his mind accounts for some of his most interesting work. He once stated that he wished to look into a painting and see the "unfathomable depth which exists in all works, leading us to see more and more, yet hiding the end ever from our reach." No better description could be given for the haunting world of his *Cupid and Psyche*. The figures are sculptural and immediate, yet seem at the same time to be elusive and immaterial; the background is a standard landscape, but one seeks in vain to find a fixed point of location. It is a darkly mysterious painting, at once rich and sensuous, but filmy and indeterminate as well. Its world is one of dislocation, of gliding among the unreal objects of a dream.

Albert Pinkham Ryder (1847-1917) has continued to loom as the dominant painter from the American past. He has exerted more influence on the twentieth century than

Nineteenth-Century
Eccentrics and
the American Tradition

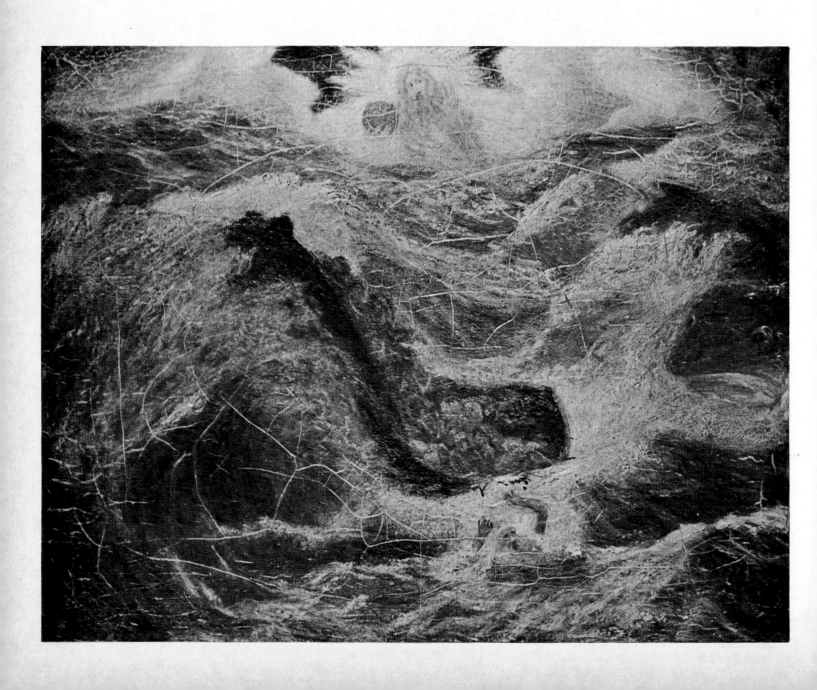

Albert Pinkham Ryder: *The Temple of the Mind* [above], ca. 1885, 17¾ inches high. Ryder wrote in 1907 that the theme was taken from Poe's poem, *The Haunted Palace* [Albright-Knox Gallery, Buffalo].

A visible God watches over his prophet: Ryder's *Jonah,* 27⅛ inches high [National Gallery, Washington, D.C.].

any other artist; Jackson Pollock stated that Ryder was the only American master who interested him, a feeling echoed by Hans Hofmann. De Kooning and Gorky each found a source of interest in his vast powers. Ryder's art embodies universal symbols that transcend any questions of nationality, yet he seems, more than any other painter, to be uniquely American if only by virtue of his sheer pictorial energy. His position has been regarded as the very emblem of the artist in this country: lonely, isolated, largely unrecognized, but maintaining an absolute and uncompromising fidelity to his belief. His art represents an extension of the quest for the most elemental and profound truths of human existence; it can be taken as fitting Coleridge's definition of art as "the subjection of matter to spirit so as to be transformed into symbols through which the spirit reveals itself."

With the exception of some brief training under William E. Marshall in the early 1870s, Ryder was entirely self-taught. He had come to New York from his native New Bedford in 1870 and had been rejected at the National Academy. Under Marshall's encouragement he applied again and was finally accepted, and exhibited there for the first time in 1873. He became associated with the Society of American Artists, which had been founded in 1877 as a rival to the Academy, and exhibited with the new group until 1887. It was only then that he began to receive any critical attention at all. Ryder's paintings of the 1870s were generally landscapes of an idyllic mood, set in a late afternoon atmosphere, and usually painted directly from nature. A short trip to England in 1877, and an extended visit to England, France, Holland, Italy, Spain and Tangier in 1882, were important to the development of his mature style. In Holland he saw the work of Matthew Maris, the painter who exerted the single most important influence on his art. Ryder exhibited only once after 1887, and from this point on he became more and more of a recluse. Living an utterly solitary life after 1900, Ryder spent his last years working and reworking old paintings, and never undertaking any new canvases.

Ryder's choice of themes emphasizes the vital role that myth assumed in his art. The sources he drew on—Shakespeare, the Bible, Chaucer, Byron, Poe, Tennyson and Wagner, among others—all contain elements that refer to the confrontation of man with the unseen forces by which he is continually shaped. Through the elements of myth and ritual, time-less statements are expressed about his relation to those forces, whether they be natural, religious or psychic. Ryder's art conveys, either by the cosmic energies of the *Jonah,* or by the haunting mystery of *The Temple of the Mind,* the fears, drives and aspirations which form the core of man's experience. The emotive power of his work carries one beyond the specific into a world of a primeval and unceasing drama. But in this oblique world of arbitrary and laden forms, it is the inexplicable, the enigmatic and ultimately indefinable which continues to intrigue us, as elusive as existence itself.

The painting of Robert Loftin Newman (1827-1912) relates to that of Ryder, but contains none of his metaphysical depths. Newman's themes were almost always taken from the Bible, and although they are shrouded in a certain aura of veiled secrecy, his

Nineteenth-Century Eccentrics and the American Tradition

William Page's *Cupid and Psyche* [above], 1843 [10⅞ inches high; private collection], is a uniquely mysterious and haunting work by an otherwise rather pedestrian painter. Perhaps it reflects his preoccupation with Swedenborgian metaphysics.

Portrait of Mrs. Blakelock [left; Victor Spark Collection, New York] and *The Vision of Life* [below, right; 21 inches high; Chicago Art Institute], by Ralph Blakelock (1847-1919), who became fascinated by Far West land-scapes and Indian life, turning them into idiosyncratic symbols.

145

Robert Loftin Newman (1827-1912): *Saul
and the Witch of Endor;* "a process of
working and revealing to discover a
tenuous and shifting order beneath
its surface" [Graham Gallery, New York].

real interest lies in his handling of paint. He had gone to Europe in 1850, and again in 1854, at which time he met Millet and William Morris Hunt and spent several months at Barbizon. After his return he settled in the South, where he had been born and raised. He was conscripted by the Confederate Army when the Civil War broke out; at the end of the war he came to New York and settled there for the rest of his life. His work was not shown in any quantity until 1894, and his isolation was made complete by the fact that he lived as a virtual recluse. He is, by comparison with Ryder or Blakelock, a minor painter, but at his best, he achieved an orchestration of color of impressive accomplishment. The love of surface and the sensuous qualities of paint itself is rare in American art before 1945. Newman was one of the few painters in whom one can discern the willful manipulation of pigment to find its expressive possibilities. His rich, vibrant color shows a process of working and revealing, to discover a tenuous and shifting order beneath its surface. This process is clearly evident; no effort is made to conceal the struggle to realize a pictorial balance. As a result his work has an awkward and unfinished look, but the resulting freedom of movement for line, mass and color achieves a vigorous and sustained expressiveness.

Ralph Blakelock (1847-1919) found in the forest, as Ryder had in the sea, a haunting symbol of the mysteries and undisclosed terrors of the unknown. Like his contemporary, Ryder, he was self-taught. His early work consisted mostly of precise, literal landscapes in the tradition of the Hudson River School. Although he never went abroad, his career was decisively affected by a long journey to the Far West begun in 1869. During his three years in the wilderness Blakelock came to be fascinated by Indian life, and often used such motifs in his work. After his return to the East he found himself beset by increasingly desperate financial circumstances. With a large family to support he was forced to sell what few paintings he could for next to nothing. The pressure of his circumstances

Nineteenth-Century Eccentrics and the American Tradition

Erastus Salisbury Field's *Historical Monument to the American Republic,* ca. 1876, intended by Field to be erected on the site of the Philadelphia Centennial Exposition [9 feet, 3 inches high; Museum of Fine Arts, Springfield, Mass.].

HISTORICAL MONUMENT OF THE AMERICAN REPUBLIC.

finally broke him, and in 1899 he was committed to an asylum for the insane where he spent most of his remaining years, unable to paint. Tragically, soon after his commitment he began to receive critical acclaim and a substantial rise in the value of his paintings soon followed.

By 1880 Blakelock had discarded his precise linear style for a submerged nocturnal world of the suggested and implied. For the next twenty years he concentrated more and more on pure landscapes to the exclusion of Biblical, literary or mythological themes. Blakelock once stated that, "color should flow upon the senses, as some melody," and in his painting he generally keyed his color scheme to a dominant tone which sets the emotional tenor and ambience. Color does not flow in the sense that it does in Ryder and Newman—in broad, sweeping strokes that pull together areas and shapes. For Blakelock color was to be applied in broken touches to give the effect of a sequence of tightly etched and defined patterns. His motivation was frequently touched off by patterns suggested to him by the grain of boards and the surface of cracked bathtub enamel. This feeling of peering into the arabesques of a highly textured surface gives Blakelock's paintings an alternation between the intricate and the expansive, between the confined and the limitless, and imbues them with a complexity and life of their own.

Although his work was for the most part portraiture, Erastus Salisbury Field (1805-1900) did do a series of purely imaginative works, of which the most startling—and truly eccentric—is the *Historical Monument to the American Republic,* 1876. Field was born in Massachusetts and spent most of his life there with the exception of a few months study with Samuel F. B. Morse in New York. The *Historical Monument* was conceived on the occasion of the Philadelphia Centennial Exposition, and was fully intended by Field to be erected on the site of the exposition. The painting itself shows nine towers rising on drums and supported by colonnaded arcades set in a park filled with fountains. The seven exposition towers at the top are connected by steel bridges over which trains were to carry visitors. The platforms of the main towers are labeled "TTB" (The True Base), on which the history of the United States was portrayed in sculpture and relief. The small tower directly in the center, marked as the Tower of the Constitution, is dedicated to the memory of Abraham Lincoln. Other panels were inspired by history paintings such as Trumbull's *Signing of the Declaration of Independence* and the *Surrender of Cornwallis at Yorktown,* and Benjamin West's *Penn's Treaty with the Indians.* Field was apparently a God-fearing man, for an essay on the Bible was imprinted on the façade base of the right tower, and in a pamphlet he published he declared that the meaning of the eagles on the third tower could be found in Revelations. Precedents for the fantastic scheme can be found in the exotic architectural paintings of John Martin which had influenced Field's earlier work. Field was undoubtedly approaching insanity when he painted the *Monument*; yet it remains a unique compendium.

William Rimmer (1816-1879) may well be the most undervalued and least appreciated American artist of the nineteenth century. He is known primarily for his sculpture, and while that part of his œuvre is of great interest, it has hidden the extraordinary qualities of his painting and drawing. Half-mad and totally eccentric, Rimmer displayed a wide range of talents. He was a self-taught physician, an anatomist, teacher and lecturer as well as a painter and sculptor. He was born in England and had come to Boston with his family when only ten years old. The family lived in total isolation and dire poverty, for his father believed himself to be heir to the throne of France and waited his call to power. Rimmer himself believed his father's claim and fully shared his anguish. At the age of 14 he did a portrait of his father which he titled *Despair,* and in 1861 a statue called *Falling Gladiator* to symbolize his father's death. Rimmer had first tried an artist's career as an itinerant portraitist, but meeting with no success had begun to study medicine and later became a successful teacher of anatomy. The combination of training in anatomy, medicine and art gave him an almost surreal grasp of human movement. His drawing, *A Dead Soldier,* is an image of such anatomical immediacy as to assume an almost psychopathic intensity. The hand is thrust against the frame with terrifying reality; it is a glimpse of the anguish of death that offers no respite to one's memory or eye. Rimmer's telescoped view is emblematic of the awful facts of life and death. "We live in this world," he said, "not by let, but by opposition." In his painting *Flight and Pursuit,* we feel the reverberations of an inner clash of the mind and conscience. Plainly, two aspects of the same man are presented; each figure echoes the movements of the other, and the repetition of the similar architectural elements into infinite depth heightens the hallucinatory effect. But

Nineteenth-Century Eccentrics and the American Tradition

William Rimmer's mysterious depiction of the pursuer chasing his own psychic shadow: *Flight and Pursuit,* 1872. An admiration for Fuseli's haunted art is apparent [Boston Museum].

Index

Page numbers in italics indicate colorplates

Advertisements

Grandville: *Art Gallery.*

PARKE-BERNET GALLERIES · INC

Affiliated with SOTHEBY & CO., *London*

980 **MADISON AVENUE** • **NEW YORK, N.Y.** 10021

Public Auction Sales of Art and Literary Property

One of the Rubinstein Exhibition Galleries April 1966

The 1965-66 season at Parke-Bernet Galleries gross sales totalled $23,519,367 and was notable for the large number of important collections from single owners. Outstanding was the dispersal of the Collections of Madame Helena Rubinstein auctioned during nine sessions (including her jewelry) which attained a total of $2,958,217

Subscriptions to Parke-Bernet *and/or* Sotheby & Co. Catalogues and Price Lists now run for a twelve month period. Order form giving rates will be sent on request

To keep informed about forthcoming sales, ask to be placed on our gratis mailing list to receive monthly *Bulletin*

SOTHEBY'S OF LONDON, Ltd. 9777 **Wilshire Blvd. Beverly Hills, Calif.**

Miss Philippa Calnan, representative, is available there to provide information for clients about sales in London and New York Telephone (213) 274-7329

The Arleigh Gallery

contemporary art

Jacques Fabert
Jean Hyson
Gloria Brown
Edward Handelman
Masatoyo Kishi
Vincent Perez
Ivan Majdrakoff
Clayton Pinkerton
Jack Kamesar
Julia Pearl
James Monte
Louis Gutierrez
Bella Tabak Feldman
Gerald Gooch
Daniel Shapiro
Helen Breger

1812 Pacific Ave.   San Francisco

OLD & MODERN MASTER PRINTS & DRAWINGS

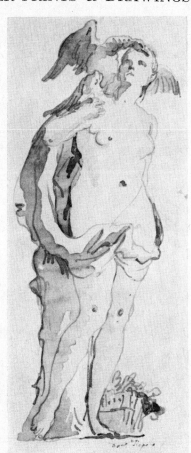

*New catalogue folio,
over 100 illustrations,
some in color. $4.00*

WILLIAM H. SCHAB GALLERY
48 EAST 57th ST., NEW YORK PLaza 8-0327

156

FIRST IMPORTANT EXHIBITION OF
FLOWER PAINTINGS by FANTIN-LATOUR

For the benefit of the BOYS' CLUB OF NEW YORK
(Catalogue available 30 color illustrations $2)

NOVEMBER 3 - DECEMBER 3

ACQUAVELLA
Galleries inc.

119 EAST 57th STREET, NEW YORK   PL 3-1296

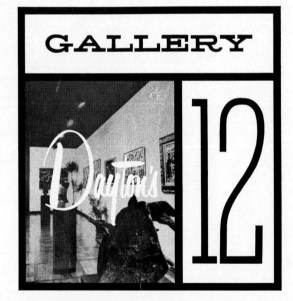

GRAHAM

Established in New York since 1857

1014 Madison Avenue, New York

EDWIN DICKINSON

Still - Life With Flowers   1938

AMERICAN
PAINTINGS & DRAWINGS
1750-1966

"La Ferme Bretonne" Oil 29" x 39" by Georges Le Meur 1965

BURGOS GALLERIES Ltd.

*Fine Contemporary
Paintings and Sculpture*

127 East 57 Street, New York, N.Y.　　　*TE 8-0017*

New York　•　Southampton　•　Montego Bay

contemporary

painting

and

sculpture

POINDEXTER

21 W. 56

prized!

A fine water color brush is prized by the artist...it feels right in his hand, it points readily, it springs back, it responds to his every mood and demand—a fine delicate line...a bold splash of color! Such a brush is WINSOR & NEWTON's Pure Red Sable **Series 9.** Surpassed only by WINSOR & NEWTON's incomparable Series 7, **Series 9** are designed for the artist who wants a fine watercolor brush at a lower price. **Series 9** brushes are set in cupro-nickel seamless ferrules and mounted in polished walnut handles. Sizes include 000-12, priced from **$.65 to $18.50**

illustration actual size

On sale at leading art material dealers.

Winsor & Newton Inc.
881 Broadway, New York, N.Y. 10003
Canadian Agents: The Hughes Owens Co., Ltd., Montreal
Californian Dist.: The Schwabacher-Frey Co., San Francisco, Los Angeles

161

LARRY ZOX

KORNBLEE GALLERY   58 EAST 79 STREET   NEW YORK

ANTIQUE AND MODERN
PICTURE FRAMES

Finest Collection of
Antique Picture Frames

repairing
restoring
regilding

J. H. GUTTMANN

148 EAST 57 STREET, NEW YORK
MU 8-3940

FleischerAnhaltGallery
Chuey
Dimondstein
Gebhardt
Lubner
742¼ north
LaCienega boulevard
Los Angeles
90069
213 657 4038

OLD AND NEW AT THE

ALLAN STONE GALLERY

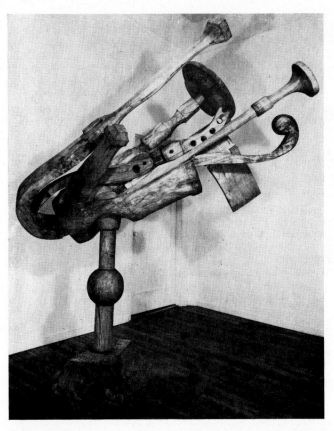

John Anderson

Joseph Cornell

Wayne Thiebaud

Robert Mallary

48 EAST 86TH STREET, NEW YORK, N.Y.

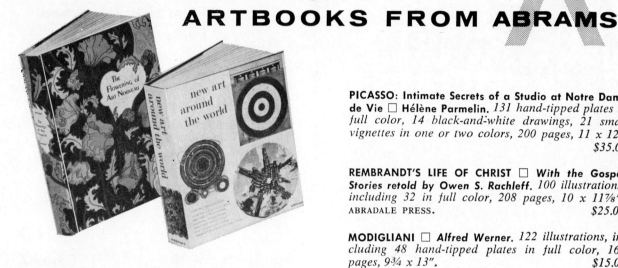

JUAN VAN DER HAMEN
(Madrid, 1596–1632)

On canvas, size 22 by 41 inches
Fully signed and dated 1623

NEWHOUSE GALLERIES

Established 1878

15 EAST 57th STREET, NEW YORK, N. Y.

PLaza 5-4980

CLEVELAND
institute of art

PROFESSIONAL TRAINING

Painting	Ceramics
Sculpture	Weaving
Printmaking	Textile Design
Graphic Design	Silversmithing
Industrial Design	Enameling
Photography	Teacher Training

DEGREES-SCHOLARSHIPS-CATALOG ON REQUEST

Write: Director of Admissions, 11141 East Boulevard,
Cleveland, Ohio 44106

G. B. Tiepolo   "Portrait of an Oriental"

•

DRAWINGS, PASTELS & WATERCOLORS

Contemporary French Tapestries

•

CHARLES E. SLATKIN, INC. GALLERIES

115 East 92nd Street   New York

LE 4-4222

pierre matisse gallery
4I e 57 street new york 22

balthus, dubuffet,

giacometti, butler,

calliyannis, miró,

marini, macIver,

riopelle, roszak,

saura, millares, rivera,

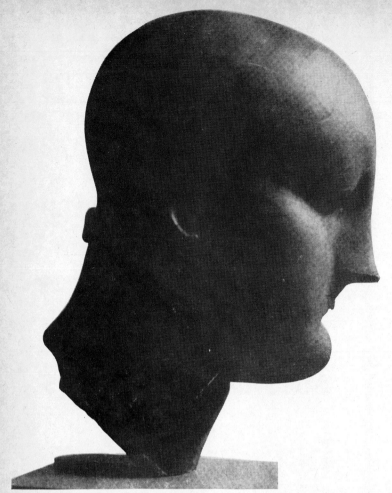

Head of a Man   c1909   Bronze   Elie Nadelman
Reproduced --- Page 18 "Sculpture of Elie Nadelman" by Lincoln Kirstein

GREER GALLERY

35 West 53, New York, CI 6-1555

Recent Acquisitions

Cassatt

De Chirico

Ernst

Foujita

Lipshitz

Luks

Marsh

Masson

Pougny

Soutine

Tanguy

Toulouse Lautrec

&

Sculpture by Zadkine

---

cordier & ekstrom

978 madison ave., new york

October:

H.-E. KALINOWSKI

November:

WALTER DE MARIA

December:

MONO-IMAGISTS

January:

RICHARD LINDNER

EUGENE DELACROIX: Etude de Femme, vué de dos. Etching 1833. Delteil 21 i/iv. The extremely rare first state from the collections of A. Beurdeley and Henri Delacroix.

IMPORTANT ORIGINAL PRINTS

NEW CATALOGUE AVAILABLE

PETER DEITSCH GALLERY

24 E. 81   REgent 7-8279

Vice-President in charge of good taste:

If a man wants
to put up a
building
in the shape of an
elephant,
there are just two
restraints that can
prevent such a
monstrosity:
(1) A strong building code,
(2) An adviser with a sense
of good taste.
When man uproots nature,
taking away trees, flowers,
rocks and beauty,
he has an obligation to do
something beautiful in return.
Monotonous look-alike housing
developments are not enough.
Cigar-box buildings are not enough.
Public housing projects, lined up like
file drawers are not enough.
Tasteless, hungry developers
will build anything as long
as you'll buy it.
Governments, business firms,
clubs and families should appoint
a Vice-President in charge of
good taste.
Then someday "American Beauty"
will stand for
An American Rose,
An American Woman,
An American Building.

This
message
is from...

Newsweek

George Braque   1882-1964
Les Pommes Jaunes — 1953
8" x 13"
Reproduced —Maeght Vol. 1948 — 52, pg. 71

*The Findlay Galleries specialize in contemporary
European paintings. Because we spend three months
every year in Europe searching and buying
we enjoy one of the most carefully selected
collections of contemporary art in the world.*

We have the largest collection in the world in French
primitive paintings: Bombois — Bauchant — Vivin.

A permanent collection of works by the major 19th and
20th century masters is always available.

**Delacoix — Degas — Monet — Bennard — Braque
Picasso — Chagall — Klee — Kandinsky — Jawlensky
Utrillo — Vlaminck**

Helping to start collections is our business.

Maurice Brianchon — contemporary
Bouquet de Zinias — 1962
36" x 26"

Andre Bauchant   1873-1958
Marche de St. Jean — 1946
39" x 29"

FINDLAY
GALLERIES   11 EAST 57th STREET, NEW YORK

Moment of Truth
by Nathaniel Kaz

Adam & Eve
by Clivia Morrison

Portrait of Jules Stein
by Jacques Lipchitz

The Pope
by Bruno Lucchesi

FINE BRONZE ART CASTINGS

Specializing in casting single pieces to large editions in bronze and stainless, using the Shaw Process, for professional sculptors, art schools, amateurs and museums.

For further information and brochure write to:

AVNET - SHAW ART FOUNDRY
91 Commercial Street, Plainview, New York

Maurice Prendergast

The Red Parasol
Watercolor 11″ x 15¼″

AMERICAN ARTISTS

Albert Bierstadt	Enrico Glicenstein	George Luks	T. Robinson
Frank Boggs	Childe Hassam	Willard Metcalf	Everett Shinn
Robert Brackman	Robert Henri	A. J. Miller	John Sloan
C. K. Chatterton	Thomas Hill	Grandma Moses	Joseph Stella
A. B. Davies	F. Tenney Johnson	S. A. Mount	Robert Street
E. W. Deming	William Keith	J. Francis Murphy	Thomas Sully
Louis Eilshemius	Ernest Lawson	Waldo Pierce	F. J. Waugh
William Glackens	Hayley Lever	M. Prendergast	. . . and others

NEXT DOOR TO NEW WHITNEY MUSEUM

CHAPELLIER
established 1916

943 MADISON YU8-8430
(Moving soon to our own
building at 22 E. 80th Street.)

REUBEN NAKIAN

The Trojan Woman   Plaster for Bronze 9' high

EGAN GALLERY
41 EAST 57 STREET NEW YORK 22, N. Y.

Morris Broderson   Fall River Legend Series 1966

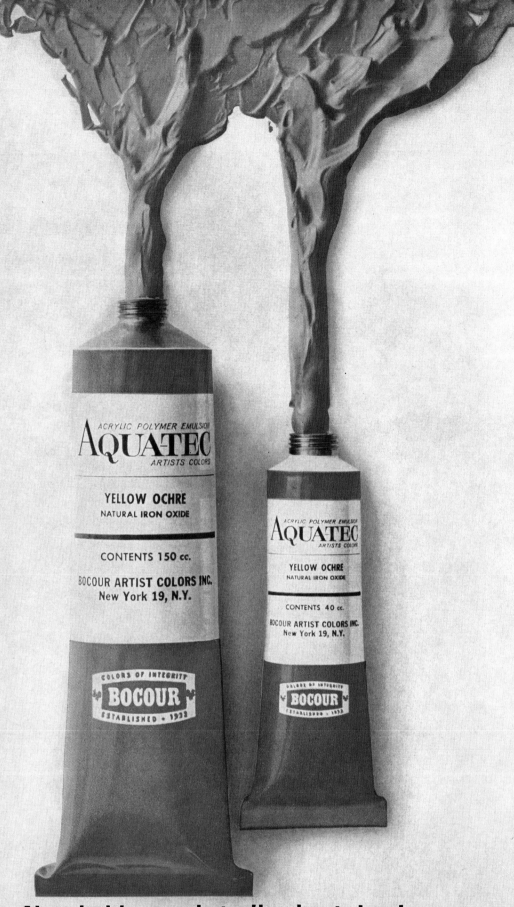

Now in king and studio size tubes!

Aquatec is a water-based artist color, made with 100% acrylic polymer emulsion. It is the finest, most versatile, color-rich medium an artist can use. Developed to provide free and expressive new techniques from thin wash to heavy impasto, without fear of darkening or cracking. It comes to you from Bocour, America's originator of acrylic resins for artist use. Take advantage of our special introductory tube offer: a working palette of 11 studio-size colors, plus Aquatec Jel and a king-size tube of Titanium White, only $6.75.* Check or money-order ...no COD's. For full information on how to use Aquatec, write Bocour Artist Colors, Inc., 552 W. 52nd St., N.Y. 10019.

AQUATEC is available at all leading art supply stores everywhere.

N.Y.C. RESIDENTS ADD 5% SALES TAX.